How To Build
Shaker Furniture

How To Build Shaker Furniture

Thos. Moser

With Measured Drawings
by Christian Becksvoort

DRAKE PUBLISHERS INC.
NEW YORK · LONDON

Published in 1977 by
Drake Publishers, Inc.
801 Second Avenue
New York, N.Y. 10017

Typography, format and book design by Harold Franklin

Art Director: Harold Franklin
Art Staff: Diane Fasano
               Amy Horowitz
               Michael Mekeel

LC: 76-46809

ISBN: 0-8473-1493-6 (Cloth)
       0-8473-1468-5 (Paper)

Printed in the United States of America

Contents

VI   Contents

Introduction

Since the advent of the Industrial Revolution the machine has increasingly placed its redundant stamp on our furniture, our houses, our clothing—all those manufactured goods that fill our daily lives. While mass production has blessed us with a cornucopia of consumer products and enriched the lives of everyone, there remains a longing for the imprimatur of the human hand.

In recent years the international craft movement has instilled a new awareness and a sense of discrimination and appreciation in untold millions. Increasingly, more people, particularly the aware young, are demanding greater craftsmanship in their furniture. The consumer wearies of planned obsolescence and looks instead for furnishings which will have use for generations to come. For many the search has led to direct participation; they have become makers, not just buyers.

Along with greater integrity in construction the search is for natural materials, uniqueness, and purity of design. Fashionability, whether it be in automobiles or furniture, has a life expectancy of five or eight years, no more. In furniture styling, since 1960, we have gone from blond oak veneer to Danish Modern to Spanish Provincial to Mediterranean foam-injected plastic to butcherblock to Western Colonial. And with each new trend the old one is quickly discarded and accused of being "dated," somehow old-fashioned and therefore no longer serviceable.

Many yearn for the timelessness of truly excellent design; for a style which communicates permanence, visual delight, integrity; for a style in harmony with natural material. The best in period furniture and the best in contemporary design satisfy these criteria. So does the style created by the early nineteenth-century Shakers.

By today's standards the Shakers lived a rigid, austere, almost monastic existence; yet it was this very dedication to simplicity that spawned an incredibly prolific (albeit brief) period of creativity in three-dimensional design unequaled in the American experience up to that point.

The early Shaker's commitment to functionalism preceded by nearly a century the clean, unadorned forms of the Bauhaus and the International School. The unornamented purity of line, the respect for wood, the overriding utility inherent in this early work, make its acceptance universal. As with the best offerings of all ages these forms transcend the assaults of time and fortune.

The designs contained herein descend from that Shaker tradition which flourished such a long time ago, yet which has direct relevance to us pressing toward the twenty-first century. These designs are not copies of antiques. They are not slavish redundancies. They are, rather, an attempt at perpetuating one small aspect of a vision which fell prey to economic and stylistic pressures 125 years ago. I would like to think that the furniture pieces described here represent a continuation and, if boldness is permitted, an improvement on what I have called "the Shaker style."

Throughout, attention is given to producing a wide range of furniture using the same building methods used by the early Shakers and by cabinetmakers of even earlier times. Although there is much discussion of machining, the age-old methods of hand craftsmanship are stressed. In this way the maker imbues his work with the touch of the hand, giving it a hallmark not found in machine production.

This book is written, not for the critic, not for the idle appreciator, but rather, for the builder, the maker. While not pretending to be a definitive volume on the art of joinery, it nevertheless offers a short course on tools and woodworking methods. The fifty or so pieces described here have all been built in our shop in New Gloucester, Maine. Some pieces have been built only once, others many times. They are all designed to be built one at a time following the same discipline used a hundred, indeed a thousand, years ago. Some pieces are near facsimilies of early Shaker work; most, however, are adaptations which have a genesis in the "mood" of the Shaker style. The methods of joinery follow those practiced by yesterday's cabinetmakers. Emphasis is placed on the use of wooden joints rather than steel fasteners. Plywood and composition board are absolutely banished. Each of these projects is so designed that it can be built entirely with hand tools, with a few basic power tools, or with a completely equipped modern shop. There is nothing sacrosanct about the dimensions or the materials, and the craftsman is urged to inject his vision, his individuality into his work.

In writing this book I express an indebtedness to those nameless joiners who worked in wood so long ago, before plastics or petroleum or automation. For in building with integrity, in building so as to make it last a thousand years, they have been my mentors. Their work remains a testament to their commitment to excellence.

Acknowledgments

Special appreciation must be extended to Steven Foster and the Shakers of Sabbathday Lake, Maine, who were so kind in providing the pictures of their truly magnificent collection; Nick Roth, master craftsman and builder of fine wooden boats; Sam Pennington of the *Maine Antiques Digest*; Bill Huston, cabinetmaker and advisor; Edwin Boyker, cabinetmaker, friend, and teacher; my wife Mary, who has taught me most of what I know about good taste; and Chris Becksvoort, cabinetmaker and artist, whose pen-and-ink drawings give special value to this effort.

Thos. Moser
New Gloucester, Maine
1977

How To Build
Shaker Furniture

Chapter 1

The Shaker Style

The Creative Process

The creative process does not take place in a vacuum. Certain remembrances are at play when a craftsman designs a piece of furniture, a certain vocabulary is used in producing the form. The language he speaks, all those three-dimensional designs he has lived in, on, or near, indeed his whole past and present, are the wellsprings of his creativity. It was Ulysses who said, "I am part of all that I have seen, and all I have seen is a part of me." In a sense, it can be argued that there is no such thing as pure creativity, that at best we can recreate with a slight improvement here or there. Design is synthesis, the reordering of existing parts into a new whole. This process is universal. The Egyptian craftsman of funeral boxes, the unknown Renaissance cabinetmaker, Thomas Jefferson in laying out the University of Virginia—all were synthesizers who borrowed images from their surroundings and produced forms of utility and joy.

As a designer and builder of furniture I see myself as a synthesizer. The drawings and photographs contained herein represent a blending of antique Shaker forms and contemporary forms. None of these are totally original designs, nor are they copies. I guess we are safe in saying that they are a composite, a synthesis, of the best of a number of worlds.

If we approach the study of Shaker furniture with this as a fundamental premise, a needed objectivity is attained. To understand Shaker design one must understand what the Shakers were and what their man-made visual world consisted of.

The Shakers: A Nineteenth-Century Genius

In 1774 Mother Ann Lee, founder of the Shaker sect, and eight followers traveled from Manchester, England, to the New World in search of greater freedom of religious expression. She was herself strongly influenced by the Religious Society of Friends, or Quakers. In their early years this new collectivity came to be called "Shaking Quakers," a term derived from certain movements performed in their liturgy. This name was later shortened to Shakers, although the sect is officially known as the United Society of Believers in Christ's Second Appearing. Like the Quakers, the Shakers were pacifists who avoided politics, theater, strong drink and "vain amusements" of every sort. They wore simple clothing, spoke in simple terms, lived in simple surroundings. Their way of life was clearly the antithesis of materialism. Today a single stone marks the graves of all at New Gloucester, Maine. On its face is inscribed "SHAKERS."

The earliest Shaker settlements were at Watervliet and Lebanon, New York; Hancock and Harvard, Massachusetts; and Enfield, Connecticut. Later, as the number of converts grew, settlements were established in Maine and New Hampshire. By the middle of the nineteenth century there was a total of nineteen communities extending as far west as Pleasant Hill, Kentucky.

Not unlike other sects of the period, such as the Oneida Community in upstate New York, the Amana group of Iowa, and the idealists of New Harmony, Indiana, the Shakers envisioned a religious, political, and social utopia. Celibacy, communal ownership of property, and a reverence for perfection in work characterized their lives. It is all but impossible for us in the twentieth century to understand, let alone empathize with, this pervasive selflessness. Yet in this chapter of American history, Shakerism flourished, both spiritually and economically. The Shakers achieved a social order based upon equality, sharing, and personal anonymity. At the heart of the creed was Christ's Second Coming, for, as set down by Mother Ann Lee, Christ was ever present within the soul of each member and within the community *per se*. This presence is made manifest in all aspects of Shaker life, particularly in the products of their craftsmanship. Her admonitions, "Put your hands to work and your hearts to God," and "Do your work as though you had a thousand years to live, and as if you were to die tomorrow," serve as a philosophico-religious basis for a high level of perfection in craftsmanship. The overriding characteristics of Shaker work are unity and simplicity. Unity of material and function bespeak the functionalism of a much later day where order and system are the cornerstones. To the Shakers, ornamentation of any sort was considered vanity, useless ostentation. Simplicity, simplicity, simplicity.

This adherence to economy of form had its detractors outside the community. Upon visiting a Shaker room at Mt. Lebanon, Charles Dickens wrote, "We walked into a grim room, where several grim hats were hanging on grim pegs and the time was grimly told by a grim clock." Had Dickens been born a hundred years later, he might well have used another, less pejorative adjective, for he saw Shakerism from a Victorian's perspective, which was colored by burdensome levels of ornamentation.

What is most awesome is the sheer volume of Shaker inventiveness. They are reputed to have invented the automatic washing machine, the circular saw, the steel pen, water-repellent clothing, the one-piece clothespin, the self-feeding surface planer, and much more. How was it that a movement consisting of fewer than six thousand souls at its height, around 1850, could produce such a prodigious array of inventions, machinery, foodstuffs, medicines, and products for farm and home?

To the followers of Mother Ann, time "was the taskmaster of toil." The artifacts left by the collective genius of the Shakers are testimony to their abiding need for efficiency as well as self-sufficiency. Few things were purchased from "the world," and in the early days few things were sold. As their numbers and strength grew, of course, commerce led them to greater levels of economic assimilation. Indeed, it was this assimilation, and the advent of true industrialism, that sounded their death knell in the twentieth century.

Today, the Shaker community consists of only ten members, and they function as repositors and custodians of the movement that once was. The surviving few, now residing in Canterbury, New Hampshire, and Sabbathday Lake, Maine, have voted to discontinue admitting new membership, and so Shakerism is truly a movement out of America's past.

Indeed, as a relevant contemporary religious and economic force, the sect has only minor influence now. However, the artifacts left by this relatively small group have never before so captivated and moved us.

Shaker Antiques

In the last thirty years Shaker furniture has been "discovered." Any discussion of American decorative arts now includes a section on Shaker design, and no comprehensive American museum of any size could function without a Shaker Collection. Indeed, just last year my wife and I visited the American Museum in Bath, England, and much to our delight we found there one of the most exquisite collections of early nineteenth-century Shaker furniture and household tools. The warm reception of this style by the English attests to its international appeal. This receptivity is shared by the Japanese, who are enchanted by these clean, uniform lines.

In the antiques market Shaker items command unheard-of prices. Recently, at an auction dedicated exclusively to Shaker artifacts in Kezar Falls, Maine, an ordinary grain sack bearing the Shaker name was reportedly sold for $240. Sets of the small wooden oval boxes which were produced in New Gloucester scarcely a generation ago are now selling for hundreds and hundreds of dollars. I remember hearing the story that after World War II an entire meetinghouse full of Shaker chairs was put to the torch because they were considered unmarketable. Today an authentic Shaker chair fetches upwards of $800.

Two years ago we contributed a small round stand of our manufacture to a local television auction. The auctioneer, thinking at first it was an original Shaker piece, exclaimed that the bidding should start at $1,400. The table, because it was not of Shaker origin, sold for one tenth that amount.

One cannot visit an antique shop without finding a horde of so-called Shaker collectables. In just one issue of an antiques magazine published here in Maine no fewer than seventeen furniture items were advertised as being "genuine" Shaker. Enormous prices, coupled with a real dearth of supply, have caused many an

A remarkable collection of original Shaker furnishings in the American Museum in Bath, England. (By permission of the American Museum in Britain, Bath)

eager antique dealer and collector to see Shaker where there is none. To have produced such a voluminous array of furniture in a period of thirty years or so, and for these many examples to have survived a hundred years of fires, flood, and other calamities, 60,000 Shakers would have had to work twenty-four hours a day building Shaker tables, boxes, clocks, and so on, and painting them in the old red!

Most of this mislabeled furniture is neither reproduction nor fake. It is, rather, an assortment of pieces made of the same materials and at approximately the same time in approximately the same style as the Shaker originals. In other words, with a few exceptions, Shaker furniture is to a great extent indistinguishable by most non-

experts from other country-made primitives of the period.

The Origins of Shaker Design

In order to understand how this could happen one must remember that the Shakers were celibates, and as such no new members could be born into the church. Growth was predicated upon propagation, not procreation. And although many of the converts were brought up from childhood in the Shaker communities, the preponderance came from the outside world as adults, adults replete with trades and traditions. To be sure, most were farmers, but some were also carpenters. And the best carpenters became cabinetmakers and chairmakers. Many of the Shaker joiners had their apprenticeships in secular cabinetmaking

Shaker boxes, stools, and cupboards. (Maine Antiques Digest, Courtesy Avis Howells Antiques, Belfast, Maine)

Shakers Seeds labels — eleven of these (one was damaged) sold at an auction for $200 in October 1976. (Maine Antiques Digest)

shops whose masters knew nothing of Shakerism. As such, they learned the art of joinery from master artisans who were themselves strongly influenced by styles and trends of the time. Naturally, when these builders joined the church, they carried these tastes and styles with them.

In fact, the evolution of Shaker furniture style runs more or less concurrent with the evolution of American country furniture style in general. In the cities, of course, there were large shops which produced in the grand style much of what we today call "period furniture." Designs by Thomas Chippendale were executed in New York, Philadelphia, and Newport between 1760 and 1800. After the Revolutionary War the intricate inlay work and elaborate fluting of Hepplewhite and Sheraton were produced in what is now called the Federal period, from 1780 to 1830. These period styles were copied by most cabinetmakers of the day, but the further from the city the copier, the less elaborate and ornamented the work appears. The rural builders lacked not only the skills and materials to do multichromatic inlays, for example, but also customers to sell them to. Simple rural families needed a table off of which they could eat, not a status symbol. And so we have, passed on to us over the generations, what is called Country Chippendale, Country Hepplewhite, and Country Sheraton furniture.

This legacy is characterized by simple lines, the absence of superfluous decoration, and a sturdiness of construction rather than a delicacy. While the Goddards and the Townsends and the Phyfes were building in imported solid mahogany and exotic veneers, their country counterparts were building in pine, poplar, birch, cherry and maple—woods native to America. In order to achieve the look of mahogany they often stained their work, using an oil-based wiping stain, or used buttermilk paint to seal and conceal its humble origin. Not uncommonly, they resorted to "graining," which yielded oak, mahogany, and rosewood patterns and colors. Indeed, some were so proficient that from a distance even someone who should know better may mistake pine for rosewood. The employment of grained paint and stenciling was nowhere so evident as at the Hitchcock Chair Factory in Connecticut, where, even today, birch, pine, and maple are grained to look like rosewood.

The Shaker style therefore has its origin squarely in the secular world from which it drew its practitioners. And since style changed in the "world," so, too, it changed within the sect. In the Shakers' developmental years, from 1775 to 1800, only the crudest furniture was built, and that in small amounts. The few pieces that survive are

Shaker flour sacks — two of these sold for $100 at an auction in Bolton, Massachusetts recently. (Maine Antiques Digest)

An authentic Shaker design in pine, having considerable value. (Maine Antiques Digest, Courtesy Rooster Antiques, Concord, New York)

gradually led to a conscious effort to imbue furniture designs of the period with purity and simplicity. Since order, cleanliness, and simplicity were to be ever-present in their daily actions and thoughts, it is little wonder that these principles should be manifest in their furniture and other domestic appurtenances.

The period between 1820 and 1850 was the Shakers' golden age of design, a kind of Periclean age during which pure forms spilled forth. Forms light in expression, well balanced, not excessive in any regard, were produced for domestic use. This period is also noted for its exquisite workmanship. Joints were delicately made, and the handling of wood reached perfection. Understatement and effortlessness seem to permeate much of the period. Finishes were applied with care, and still perform even today the task of stabilizing and enriching the grain.

The New Lebanon Church family, the largest eastern community, was the "fountainhead" of Shakerism. It was the home of the central ministry and also the place where the definitive Shaker form was produced. Articles made there often served as samples for the guidance of other makers in other communities, although all artisans were free to express themselves within broad church doctrine. While still bearing a resemblance to Hepplewhite and Sheraton, these forms evolved to unique dimensions. A new vocabulary in design was achieved and became a pervasive influence in exterior and interior architecture and furnishings. The starkness of white plaster rooms is broken by horizontal chair rails and pegboards. Windows and doors are trimmed using a minimum of material. Storage room is achieved by architectural built-in cupboards and drawers, and these blended with other interior features to produce a quiet eloquence. Order and cleanliness prevailed in their living, working, and worshipping spaces.

After 1850 Shaker furniture went into decline. With greater worldly intercourse came a profusion of Victorian production. The excesses of the genre steadily degraded an earlier perfection, and by the turn of the twentieth century no Shaker furniture of consequence was being produced.

Though short-lived, the early nineteenth-century golden age produced a collection of truly remarkable furniture. The complex influences of

strictly country primitives not unlike any other products of rural New England and the Upper Hudson Valley. But in their struggle to overcome worldliness, their physical and social separation

Oval boxes, step stool, and child's rocking chair — all of Shaker origin. (Maine Antiques Digest, Courtesy Rooster Antiques, Concord, New Hampshire)

religious and social systems led to the creation of a truly inspired form.

Thos. Moser, Cabinetmakers

Thos. Moser, Cabinetmakers, began producing furniture in the Shaker style as early as 1972. In the beginning a dozen or so designs from circa 1830 were built more or less as reproductions of Shaker originals. Measured drawings were consulted and followed meticulously. There is a place for copying in the development of any craftsman. For it is through faithful imitation that certain otherwise obscure principles can be learned. Any skill, be it woodworking, oratory, or surgery, can best be learned in the shadow of a master. In a sense, the designer-practitioner should be able to work within the discipline of proven or demonstrable systems of the past before he plunges blindly into the future. I lack respect for the painter who has not mastered his craft so as to be able to produce representational art even though he practices abstract expressionism or nonobjective art. All too often the college sophomore art student begins splashing about as an avowed abstractionist "expressing" a full range of emotions without first being able to mix color, achieve unity or balance, and create

disciplined form. One cannot run until one has learned to walk. Similarly, the furniture designer and cabinetmaker whose entire background begins and ends in a single contemporary idiom does himself a disservice. In developing our craft here in New Gloucester, we have built in the period style, with its exacting carving and graceful ornament; we have built contemporary forms, with laminated components; we have built architectural assemblies, doors, mantels and spiral staircases; we have made knife handles, waterwheels, wooden tools. My definition of a cabinetmaker is one who works in wood and has a broad design repertoire, but it is the wood, the medium, which sets him apart from other craftsmen. Only the inherent nature of wood limits his repertoire.

There are many ways one can learn the art. The old system of apprenticing oneself for five or seven years to a master is virtually defunct today both here and in Europe. The demands of the marketplace rule this out. Where there are apprenticeships established, production schedules and the goddess Efficiency rob the apprentice of

A beautiful display of Shaker craftsmanship. (Maine Antiques Digest, Courtesy Greenwillow Farm, Chatham, New York)

Above: Shaker tables: (top) Mt. Lebanon, New York; (middle) Sabbathday Lake, Maine; (bottom) Mt. Lebanon, New York. (Maine Antiques Digest, Courtesy King Philip Antiques, Wrentham, Massachusetts)

the time necessary to make mistakes. Apprenticeship programs within restoration projects, such as Williamsburg or Sturbridge, are conceived for the enlightenment of the viewers, not the apprentice who is often little more than an interpreter. Still, one can learn from past masters, if not directly, then at least through their work. I have disassembled, repaired, and reassembled hundreds of antiques built fifty or a hundred or three hundred years ago. These afford a kind of classroom, as it were, a chance to observe in three dimensional form the work of anonymous joiners long departed from this life. In taking apart a piece, in studying its joint system, in seeing and feeling the marks left by a backsaw and chisel, one can imagine himself at the side of the maker. I delight in experiencing this re-creative process. I wonder during what season a piece was built, for whom, where the wood came from and how it was cut, what the maker had on his mind as he labored, what time of day it was built. The joy of opening a joint that has not seen daylight since its making is like discovering an author whose notions on this topic or that are exactly like one's own. One feels a close rapport, an intimacy in communication, that is rare and to be savored.

With experience one learns to anticipate what to look for in ancient cabinetry, since the methods of joining are relatively few and, in time, become predictable. Unlike today's craftsmen, the old-timers didn't have a convenient glue and therefore used it sparingly. It is for this reason that our task of disassembly and repairing is made so much easier. I often think the eighteenth-century joiner knew that some day his work would be so exposed. Why else would he have been so precise in stamping Roman numerals on the pieces of a joint *inside* of the joint itself? Or why would he take the time to gently chamfer all the edges of a concealed tenon? When inspired, I will often write a message inside a joint or under a support or hinge in hopes that someday, years hence, somebody will read my message about Watergate or the temperament of my oldest son, Matthew.

Not all the work of the past was necessarily

Left: Primitive Shaker stand. (Maine Antiques Digest, Courtesy Peter Eaton Antiques, Newton Junction, New York)

This mahogany block-front chest was made by us and patterned after a piece built by Goddard of Newport, Rhode Island, in 1780. This is ornate Chippendale, the kind made in city shops.

This walnut slant-top desk was made by us as an example of country Chippendale. With the exception of the fancy brasses, the desk makes a simple, straightforward statement.

Rocking chair from Watervliet, New York, with rush seat, 1850. The chair is shown in the meetinghouse.

Sewing desk from Alfred, Maine, built by Elder Henry Green in the late nineteenth century.

well done. Some antiques, although they are old to be sure, are often poorly designed and occasionally poorly built. Be that as it may, I like to say I learned my art from dead men, for indeed these builders of the past are gone, but not without a trace. Their work remains, not only in the collections of fine museums, but also in antique stores and attics and homes and junk shops where it has to be exhumed from beneath thirty-two coats of paint. My greatest pleasure is to buy a basket case, a piece so badly mangled that it literally must be carried to the shop in a container. A leg, a drawer front, the painstaking removal of all but the first coat of paint, and there before the eyes of the world it stands—now a product of two builders, one dead, one living.

The pieces pictured in this book and drawn to scale had their origins in this way: they are the evolutionary result of trial and error, of textbook consultation and basket cases and many false starts. Most of these pieces have had their last design change: they are as perfect as I am able to make them. Some are still in the process of becoming. Dimensions, it seems, are always changing. We will build a chest with a 32-inch height, thereby achieving the golden mean, Aristotles' vision of perfection, only to discover that most people prefer a 34-inch height because it makes carving a turkey more convenient. In building the first "two-stepper" we followed a Shaker prototype. It turned out to be far too unstable to use with confidence. If one were to build furniture today to exactly the scale used by a Shaker community of 1830, he would be building for prepubescient children, since today's adults are fully four inches taller than Americans of 150 years ago. Similarly, table heights, chair widths, place-setting intervals, counter heights, book size, window sill elevations, chair rails, kitchens, have become somewhat standardized. In arriving at these designs, standard contemporary practices are taken into account to make each piece as usable as possible.

Also taken into account is the availability of wood in precut and dressed sizes. To be sure, the designer should be committed only to function when conceiving a form, but an ideal form that cannot be built because the materials do not exist or are too costly remains forever an ideal and not a reality. As discussed in Chapter 2, the lumber

Bed and washstand, Ministry Shop. The bed
was built in red oak at Groveland, New York,
and the stand at Hancock, in the late nineteenth
century. The Victorian influence is very
evident.

Hallway of the Meeting House, Sabbathday
Lake, Maine.

The meeting room at Sabbathday Lake. The
woodwork is a dark blue against chalk-white
walls.

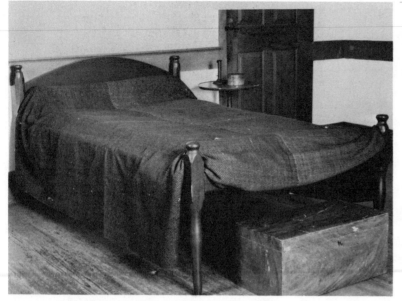

Bed built in the 1830s at Sabbathday Lake, Maine. The small box is "grained" in paint.

A writing desk from Alfred, Maine, circa 1830. The back spindles of the revolver stool, from Mt. Lebanon, are made of steel.

A built-in cupboard at Sabbathday Lake Meeting House. The two-drawer stand dates from circa 1830.

Chair and candle stand were both made at Sabbathday Lake, Maine, circa 1830.

industry has standardized dimensions to such an extent that in order for the private cabinetmaker to have a supply of all sizes he would have to either fill a warehouse or have an elaborate system of resaws and dimension planers. Therefore, most of these designs require three-quarter-inch material in commonly available widths and lengths. When smaller thicknesses are required, they can be gotten from this basic dimensional lumber. In fact, throughout, standardization is attempted in fasteners, hardware, and general dimensions.

The ladderback chairs, for example, are the product of a number of trials which have resulted in an altogether pleasing form utilizing only three spindle sizes. In fact, these same three spindles can be used to build eight different chairs. Some of the case pieces also exhibit standard size in width and depth and are designed to satisfy today's storage requirements.

The chief difference between these designs and their Shaker prototypes, aside from the dimensions, is consistency or uniformity of detail. While not conceived as an ensemble, or "suite" in the vernacular, these pieces can be built and arranged in such a way as to furnish a complete study, bedroom, or dining room, as well as occasional settings of various sorts.

The Shakers lived austere lives quite unlike our own, their functional furniture requirements were obviously quite different, and so, when necessary, preference is given to contemporary function over historical accuracy. To my knowledge, the Shakers did not make or use open-shelved cupboards; yet one is included here, although its origin is a much earlier Massachusetts pewter cupboard design. Several tables are included which are not strictly Shaker. The hutch table, with its somewhat massive base, the harvest table, and the round extension table are all basic Hepplewhite forms certainly within the Shaker sentiment, but they are not Shaker. These liberties are taken to provide a wider array of useful designs not found entirely within the collection of surviving Shaker antiques.

Moulding details, drawer pulls, and door details are also quite stylized. Similar cupboards, for example, from different communities would have displayed quite dissimilar features and it is impossible to say that one detail is more truly

A doorway on the second floor of the Meeting House, Sabbathday Lake, Maine.

Small dropleaf table made at Sabbathday Lake, Maine, in the 1840s. The chair, made in the same period, is from Alfred, Maine.

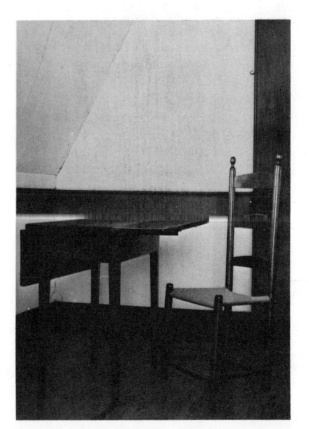

Meetinghouse peg, Sabbathday Lake, Maine.

*Detail of fingers on an oval box
from Alfred, Maine.*

Shaker than another. Experience shows that the Shaker joiner used raised, flush, and plain panels in door construction. He also used thumbnail, squared, and ridged mouldings in the door styles. Most of our designs use the raised panel and squared style because I find it most pleasing to the eye and most in conformity with the general style of the furniture in this collection.

In constructing from these drawings, the builder is encouraged to change details to suit his individual taste and need. Only proportion should hold more or less constant.

Although most of the pieces are photographed in cherry, they can also be built in another hardwood or even in pine. Indeed, most of our early work was in pine, usually painted or stained. This treatment has a rather limited appeal, however. Even among Shaker purists, painted pine does not compare with the color and richness of oiled cherry left in a natural state. Occasionally we are commissioned to build in cherry and to cover either in stain or paint. Nothing is more painful.

This collection does not lend itself to highly polished finishes. Although other kinds of finishes are occasionally used, including urethane and varnish, experience has taught us that an oil and wax treatment is by far the most satisfying in the long run.

*(All photographs on pages 10 through 14
courtesy of Sabbathday Lake Shaker Community,
photos by Stephen Foster)*

Chapter 2

Materials

A Covenant with Wood

A craftsman is but a handmaiden to his material. The inherent qualities of wood limit to a considerable extent the cabinetmaker's choices. Unlike plastic or rubber, concrete or steel, wood has a mind of its own. It is not easily bent and when bent wants to return in time to its original form. It is easy to break along its grain, yet it will withstand considerable shearing force. It warps without provocation and swells and contracts with the seasons as though it had entered a conspiracy with the calendar to loosen chair rungs in the winter and swell drawers shut in summer. Wood cracks mindlessly, can shed a finish with disastrous effect, refuses to be cut from north to south yet yields submissively from east to west. It splinters, bows, cups, shrinks, loosens, swells, dents, cracks, gives off slivers, and changes color. Yet to many of us wood remains the most pleasing of all natural materials, for in the richness and variety of its grain is to be found nature's texture incarnate. Wood is a kind of bridge between man and that organic mass of growing things he calls Mother Earth. Wood is a renewable resource which has given us warmth and shelter and provided unrivaled joy to the eye and to the touch since long before recorded time. Along with water and stone it is our most fundamental material—without it our world would be an alien place. In wood man fashioned his first tool; in wood he built the ladder with which he has ascended over the millennia. It literally surrounds us from the cradle to the coffin, and so it has been from the earliest times.

When the craftsman commits himself to work in wood, he becomes a party in a contract. If he is sensitive to his material, he enters into a kind of covenant in which he acknowledges a certain subservience to his medium. He agrees (1) to come to understand, not in a cognitive way, but through feelings, the nature of wood; (2) to admit at the very beginning that there is no such thing as perfection in wood, for in spite of all his efforts there will always be some minute blemish, some telltale error, recorded in the wood though known only to the builder; (3) in laying out and forming joints, to anticipate the inevitable movement that will occur long after the work is finished.

Classification of Wood

The two broadest classifications of wood are hardwood and softwood—misnomers both, since some species of softwood are much harder than some hardwoods. A more accurate dichotomy would be deciduous (broadleaf trees, which usually shed their foliage in autumn) and coniferous (needle-bearing trees, which appear green all year long). Typically, the texture of hardwood is much firmer, much heavier, much less easily dented, and therefore more difficult to cut and tool than softwood. Exceptions abound. Poplar, called "popel" in Maine, and basswood, both hard-woods, are considerably softer and lighter than some species of pine or other softwoods such as tamarack or hemlock. Yellow pine can be as hard as rock maple, yet it parades as a softwood.

In working with wood all my adult life I have come to be able to identify many woods, yet in spite of all my efforts there remain many which escape me: plum, dogwood, cypress, many species of pine, live oak, certain nut trees . . . the list seems endless. Now add to this the many ex-otic woods from around the world and the magnitude of the problem begins to appear. The conclusion here is that no man will ever come to know every species of wood used by the cabinet-maker. To be able to identify North American

hardwoods is accomplishment enough. And since we are concerned with the Shaker style let us con-fine our discussion to American wood species which are of value in the construction of fur-niture.

The Shakers of nineteenth-century America had at their fingertips an entire continent of virgin wood of every imaginable variety. While his European counterpart was largely limited to beech, birch, and oak, and those in a size and a quality diminished through centuries of har-vesting, the American joiner saw hardwood for-ests stretching from Florida to Maine and far beyond the Mississippi. In work which has sur-vived, it is not uncommon to find single boards 24 and 28 inches wide—free of sapwood and knots. Single trees of eastern white pine provided four thousand board feet with a butt log so clear that entire doors and tabletops were made of one slab of solid heart wood. Today a ten-foot board of black walnut twelve inches wide is stored in a safe place and only rarely brought out for viewing.

A white pine board cut from virgin timber in New Gloucester, Maine, in 1922. This board is thirty-nine inches wide and sixteen and a half feet long. It is a full inch thick. I have five such boards, but will probably never bring my-self to use them.

Clear butt logs used in the making of veneers have become so scarce that recently a single black walnut tree in southern Illinois was sold to a European veneer manufacturer for a reported $12,000.

Since most hardwood trees take from 75 to 150 years to mature, it is understandable that quality will continue to diminish while price keeps pace with increased demand.

Wood Species

Of the hundreds of species of trees that forest our land, only a relative few lend themselves to fine furniture making. Some lesser quality wood is satisfactory as a secondary wood or material that is found only inside a case piece, such as a drawer bottom or leg brace, but would hardly do on a highly visible surface.

Eastern White Pine: Of the hundreds of pine varieties, nothing equals eastern white. It can be found almost everywhere in excellent grades. Although it is commonly available as a kiln-dried wood, I prefer to work with air-cured pine. The kiln seems to kill the wood, causing it to become brittle and susceptible to a kind of internal checking or cracking. A rule of thumb in drying pine is one year to the inch. White pine tools well, is very stable and relatively strong. Small knots, if tight at the outset, will stay in place, although they are likely to bleed pitch long after they are finished. Slash knots, of course, will fall out in time. Pine is very easy to sand and will take a fairly good shine. This wood will accept a stain very evenly, although if left in a natural state or simply oiled, it will develop a warm patina in six months or so. This is particularly true of the heartwood (in early days called pumpkin pine), which is a warm orange color. The great disadvantage of eastern white pine, as of all softwoods, is that it is easily dented or scratched. Pine does not turn well, and it should probably not be used as a table or chair leg; it simply isn't strong enough. As a secondary wood pine cannot be equaled.

Western Pine: Both sugar pine and ponderosa pine have characteristics very similar to eastern pine although they are harvested only in the West

and Pacific Northwest. The great advantage of these species is that since the trees grow to such enormous size, lumber is available in widths up to thirty inches. Sugar pine is often extremely soft and has knots the size of dinner plates. In time it develops a yellow hue, especially if oiled. Ponderosa pine has a pronounced grain pattern closely resembling Douglas fir, which does not stain evenly.

White Cedar: Having many characteristics of white pine, this wood is somewhat lighter in both weight and color. Knots, even small ones, tend to fall out in time. White cedar is an extremely stable wood which is easily air dried. One additional advantage comes from the slight fragrance emanating from the wood.

Aromatic Cedar: Consistent with its name, aromatic cedar is distinguished for its strong odor, which is anathema to moths. This reddish-purple southern wood has little else to recommend it, and as far as I am concerned, it should be used only as an interior liner.

Basswood: While classified as deciduous, basswood is an extremely light wood, almost white in color. It is odorless. Its wood does not change appreciably with time. It tools well and has a very close grain. Basswood is not an attractive wood, but is an excellent secondary wood.

Poplar: Poplar is close in many respects to basswood, a little heavier, perhaps, with color ranging from greenish-blue to pink. When cut, poplar gives off a musty, unpleasant odor. It is usually found as a secondary wood, although our forefathers were known to apply a sap stain to it and pass it off as walnut. In my inventory poplar is not a popular wood.

Beech: One of the hardest of hardwoods, beech is a light tan, colors very slowly, and is often processed as bolt wood, yielding material for mallets, chisel handles, school desk tops, and wooden toys. Although the Europeans use beech to a considerable extent (it's one of their most common hardwoods), it isn't all that stable and will warp with just the threat of moisture or heat. Beech is also susceptible to rapid deterioration when left out of doors. I once air-dried a pallet of beech for two and a half years only to discover that the lower half of the pile had rotted away.

Yellow Birch: One of the cabinet woods most widely used by the early American builder was yellow birch. Harder than white birch, it also has a more interesting grain pattern. Often yellow birch is stained to look like maple, mahogany, or walnut, and more than one antique birch table has been sold as walnut. Yellow birch is quite hard, has machining properties similar to cherry, is extremely strong and commonly available in lumber yards across the country. In fact, yellow birch is probably the most easily obtained hardwood for the small cabinetmaking shop.

Rock Maple: Rock maple, also called sugar maple or hard maple, is not to be confused with the softer red or swamp maple. Being very hard and close-grained, it polishes better than any other. It has considerable compression strength and makes, in addition to rolling pins, the sturdiest chair legs. It turns beautifully on a lathe and in time develops a soft honey-colored patina. Maple is not an easy wood to work with, and the home builder is cautioned to keep his tools sharp when working with this wood. Since few people can tell the difference between maple and yellow birch, and since birch is easier to work and more readily available, for general applications the use of yellow birch is advised.

White Ash: Ash air-dries very nicely, can be rived (split) from logs rather than sawn, and is, along with hickory, the best wood for thin spindles and bent components. It has a very pronounced straight grain and therefore is flexible and bends without breaking. When rived and spoke-shaved to a paper-thin thickness, ash can be woven into chair seats, baskets, etc. Ash is a tough wood and holds up well out of doors. Its color is white with a pronounced tan grain. The porous grain portions absorb stain while the white dense wood rejects it. This results in an outrageously wild grain pattern in most stained ash pieces. As an open-grained wood, ash does not sand to a uniform finish. In overcoming this, wood filler is often used to "close" the grain. Another difficulty with this open-grained wood is

its tendency to fray or splinter on or near end-grain, making it tough to turn.

Hickory: Whatever is said of ash can be said of hickory. Its grain is straight and even more pronounced, and it, too, can bend without breaking. No doubt, the teacher in "School Days" took this into consideration when choosing the whipping rod.

Oak: There are dozens of categories of oak but the two principal species broadly used in cabinetry are white oak and red oak. While both species grow across the country, red oak is generally more common to the northern regions. White oak is preferred in marine applications since it holds up better to water and climate. Beyond this, the significant difference between the two is color. When oiled, white oak colors from light tobacco brown to deep yellow, whereas red oak almost always develops that characteristic orange hue. As an open-grained wood, oak often requires a filler in finishing and tends to extreme grain configurations. Oak is one of the most difficult woods to cure properly. It takes years of air-drying or highly specialized kiln procedures to really stabilize it. I don't like working with oak because of its tendency to split and give off splinters, but perhaps this personal bias should not influence others. Certainly this aversion was not shared by the pilgrims, American Victorians, and fifty generations of mediaeval and renaissance Englishmen. Oak is very hard and durable, planes well, is widely available, and should be experienced by any serious builder.

Black Cherry: Known in days gone by as "poor man's mahogany," cherry is to my thinking the most satisfying American hardwood to work with. It is hard, but not too hard to yield to a chisel, sawtooth, or plane with a reasonably good edge. It will take a fine sanding and polish to a satin luster. It is stable, close-grained, turns well, and, most of all, develops a rich patina faster than any other wood I know of. Although pink immediately after tooling, its color runs from honey brown to deep rich red in a matter of weeks, especially if given plenty of sunlight. Not to be confused with northern pasture cherry or pin cherry, black cherry grows now most commonly in the

The board at left is rock maple, and is closed grain. The board at right is red oak, and is open-grained.

middle or central states from Pennsylvania to Missouri. To achieve stability, cherry can be either air-cured or kiln-dried. It does take on moisture with the humid seasons but no more so than any other hardwood.

Walnut: In the categorizing of American cabinet woods, I have kept walnut for last because it is rapidly becoming scarce and should be treated with deference. At one point walnut was plentiful throughout the central region of our country. It was so plentiful in fact that in some states walnut was used in the manufacture of railroad ties. Things have changed, but not that much: last year 6,000 feet of the most beautiful black walnut was sent in a shipment to a coffin manufacturer in New Hampshire. You know where it is now! Today, straight-grained walnut is so valuable that thieves make clandestine raids at midnight and use automobile mufflers to mute their chain saws. American black walnut meets or exceeds all the criteria for a furniture-quality hardwood. In addi-

tion to its fine texture and unique color, walnut offers the bonus of fragrance. A shop never smells better than when a large walnut chest is being built. My only criticism of the wood, besides its ungodly cost, is that even when heavily oiled and waxed, walnut tends to water stain. The only cure I know is a heavy sealer like varnish, lacquer or polyurethane, but at the price of that marvelous natural texture. In spite of this, walnut remains the king of American hardwoods.

Harvesting the Forest

Several systems are used in harvesting wood suitable for furniture manufacture. The furniture industry, along with turning mills, which produce dowels, legs, spindles, and various novelties,

A bolt saw with top saw for extra wide cutting. The birch bolt is fifty-two inches long and will be used in making dowels. The carriage is operated by a foot pedal.

processes bolt wood. A bolt is a log approximately 52 inches long which yields a finished board or square four feet long. These are sawn out on a bolt saw and ripped to size on a gang saw. The wood is then stacked in pallets, which facilitates handling, and usually placed in kilns for even drying. Wood of bolt dimensions is usually not available in the retail market, but it can be obtained through inventive searching.

Lumber logs, on the other hand, are sawn in lengths from six to sixteen feet, usually at two-foot intervals. Length is determined by the characteristics found in the log as it is yarded in the forest. The lumberman looks for straight, clear sections free of knots and imperfections.

Logs are scaled (measured) at the sawmill before being sawn. The sawyer, the most impor-

tant single individual in the whole process, determines how each log is to be cut. Years ago boards and dimension lumber were sawn on up-and-down saws usually powered by water. In attics and old barns can be found the long parallel teeth marks left by the crude blade as the board inched along the carriage. Often these boards measured twenty-four inches and wider. These widths were not chosen because of aesthetic preference but because the sawyer had virgin timber of enormous proportion to begin with and ripping the wide slabs into narrower widths was difficult and expensive. Since, contrary to current belief, narrow boards were more desirable in those early years, it is not uncommon to find narrow floor boards in surviving eighteenth-century parlors while the lesser rooms in the attic are floored in 24-inch-wide pine. Currently, small mills use a circular saw, many of which utilize removable carbide teeth. These saws, having a diameter of 48 inches, are capable of cutting single boards up to 18 inches wide. When larger logs are encountered, top saws are also used to slice through the log. Many larger mills now use high-speed band saws which, if properly adjusted, cut smooth straight boards of the most uniform dimensions.

In all sawmills logs are placed on a carriage and secured by dogs. The carriage, traveling on rails, passes the blade. Since sawmills use fairly thick blades (¼'' to ⅜'') and therefore cut rather wide slices (called the kerf in a log or board), for economy the more valuable lumber is cut in heavier planks which are later re-sawn on a re-cut band saw which makes a much narrower kerf and therefore wastes much less wood. Although few mills are experienced in the method, quarter-sawing achieves the finest, most stable grain characteristics in the board. Since wood cut from a radial section of a log shrinks most uniformly, this method produces the highest quality although at the greatest cost in time and waste.

The sawyer typically cuts slabs that are from one-half inch to eight or ten inches thick. In doing this he counts, not in inches, but in quarter-inch intervals. Hence, a one-inch board is called four quarter (4/4), a 2½-inch plank is called ten quarter (10/4) and a four-inch is a sixteen quarter (16/4).

Measuring Board Feet

Lumber is inventoried and sold on the basis of ''board feet.'' As the standard unit of measurement, a board foot is a one-inch (4/4) piece of wood 12 inches wide and 12 inches long, or 144 cubic inches. If the board is 2 inches thick (8/4), one board foot can be a piece 6 inches by 12 inches. With experience, this system becomes quite simple and manageable.

It should be remembered, however, that this measurement is designated at the moment the lumber leaves the sawmill, and applies to a board

This is where it all begins — with the sawyer, the most important man in the process.

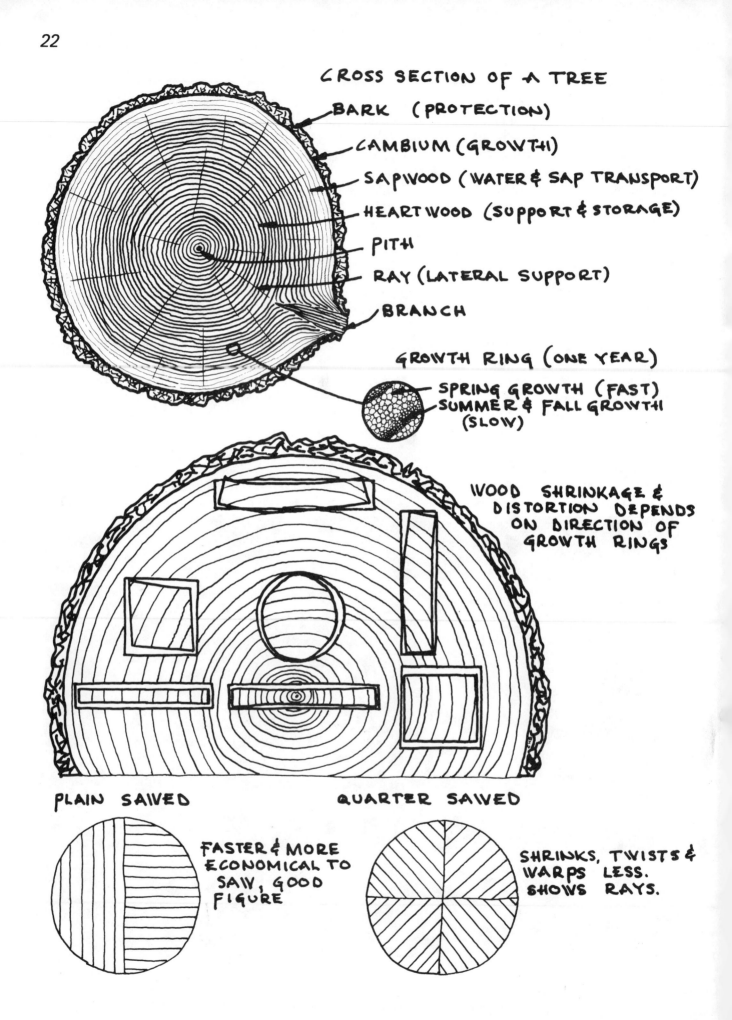

CROSS SECTION OF A TREE

BARK (PROTECTION)

CAMBIUM (GROWTH)

SAPWOOD (WATER & SAP TRANSPORT)

HEARTWOOD (SUPPORT & STORAGE)

PITH

RAY (LATERAL SUPPORT)

BRANCH

GROWTH RING (ONE YEAR)

SPRING GROWTH (FAST)
SUMMER & FALL GROWTH
(SLOW)

WOOD SHRINKAGE &
DISTORTION DEPENDS
ON DIRECTION OF
GROWTH RINGS

PLAIN SAWED

QUARTER SAWED

FASTER & MORE
ECONOMICAL TO
SAW, GOOD
FIGURE

SHRINKS, TWISTS &
WARPS LESS.
SHOWS RAYS.

even though it becomes smaller through processing. For example, let us say a 12-inch-wide birch board is cut four quarters thick and 12 feet long. It leaves the mill a designated and a true twelve board feet. Now, the board is placed in a kiln and has its moisture content reduced to 6 percent. In the process the board loses 8 percent of its volume due to natural shrinkage. The same board is now $^{15}/_{16}$ inches thick, 11⅝ inches wide and 11 feet 10½ inches long. If sold in this dry state it is still counted as twelve board feet. To further aggravate things, let's now take our board to the planing mill where it is dressed on four sides. Our board now is ¾ inch thick and 11 inches wide and 11 feet 10½ inches long—yet it is still said to be twelve board feet.

Handling and Curing Lumber

As soon as the material comes out of the sawmill it should be stacked and separated between stickers. Many woods, particularly white pine, will generate a fungus or mold if left stacked in a pile with little or no air circulation. This fungus does not affect the structure of the wood but does cause a permanent discoloration (usually blue streaks, particularly in the sapwood). Sun also causes freshly cut wood to warp and check (to crack near the ends), so the prudent mill operator will get his freshly cut lumber under cover, or at least into the shade. Stickers, one inch by one inch sticks approximately four feet long, are placed between layers of boards to facilitate air circulation. Also, one-inch gaps should be left between boards within a layer. Hardwoods should have their ends painted to decelerate end-drying and retard checking.

Climate, the season, wind, temperature, rainfall—all these affect the drying time of lumber. Most lumber dries hardly at all in winter when the cells are frozen or the lumber is buried in snow. Similarly, in May and June, with an average humidity level of 90 percent and much rain, little drying occurs. Generally, the best season for air-curing wood is late summer and fall.

To be safe, I would recommend leaving hardwood lumber out of doors, well protected from sun and rain, a minimum of two years for each inch of thickness. The wood then should come indoors and be stored in a dry area, attic or barn loft, for another month or two. If room is available, stickers should be kept in place until the material is used.

Another method of curing wood is the use of the dry kiln. Using heat, steam, and air movement, a predetermined cycle lasting from five days to six weeks is programmed into the kiln and monitored almost hourly. The technology, thermal energy, and constant monitoring make the kiln process extremely difficult and out of the reach of most small cabinet shops.

In a living tree trunk everything but the sapwood is dead. The heartwood, the preponderance of the tree's mass, serves only as vertical support, while the sapwood acts as the conduit for moisture and nutriment from leaves to roots and roots to leaves. This tissue, therefore, is heavily laden with sap and water. The cells themselves are swollen in the freshly cut wood. Before using the material in a fine tabletop, for example, the moisture content from between and within the cells must be lowered to 6 percent or 8 percent. The only way to achieve this is by evaporation, either natural or artificial.

Moisture content in freshly cut lumber ranges from 30 percent to 200 percent of the weight of wood. Proper air drying should reduce this to 10 percent or 12 percent. Efficient kilns can bring moisture down to 6 percent. When the moisture is at a level within the 6 percent to 12 percent range, we then can predict enough stability in the wood to fashion fine furniture. To use wood prematurely, while it is still green, is the folly of the inexperienced. Nothing is quite so painful as spending a week building the "perfect" table only to have it shrink, crack, and fall apart during the first winter it is used in a centrally heated home.

The experienced hand can tell if a piece of wood is dry by its feel and weight. To be absolutely sure, one can use a moisture meter. The average builder, however, is safe in using only kiln-dried lumber. Even if it has been stored for several years, it should be sufficiently dry. If air-cured wood is to be used, one should be sure enough time has passed to be safe.

One other precaution can be taken to reduce

the effect of moisture. Wood to be used in production should be brought into the shop a week or so before it is actually worked on, in order to properly condition it.

Grain Characteristics

Generally, sapwood should be avoided in cabinetry since it is often of a much lighter color and softer texture than heartwood. Along with the bark (sometimes called wane), this material is ripped and discarded when preparing the wood. Similarly, heartwood when it manifests dry heart or rot should also be stripped from the board.

The grain or visual pattern in a board is caused by the tree's capillaries, growth rings, radial rays,

A stack of 2000 board feet of eastern white pine on stickers being air dried. This wood was cut in September and will be ready for use the next August.

and, possibly, physical trauma experienced by the living tree a hundred years ago. All of these contribute to that wondrous convolution called graining. Like snowflakes, no two pieces of wood are alike. Every board has its color, its grain configuration, its own character. Naturally, the cabinetmaker matches and balances grains and sometimes builds counterpoints with the patterns.

Wood Figure

Every wood has a characteristic grain pattern which is revealed depending upon how the log is sawn. For many woods, quartersawing provides the most attractive graining and the most stable lumber, although it certainly wastes more wood.

Some woods, such as birch and cherry, exhibit a kind of feather pattern in certain boards. Other woods, particularly maple, occasionally exhibit tiger striping or bird's-eye patterns. It is impossible to predict these patterns by examining the log

before it is sawn; consequently, their discovery stands at par with the opening of King Tut's tomb. Since extreme figuring is considered a defect by the large furniture manufacturers, who employ automatic lathes and other machines, the finest graining is often thrown away as cull wood. Interesting grain patterns can also be found in wood cut near roots, large knots, and crotches or Y's in the tree.

The best way to preview what a given piece of wood will look like when finished is to wet it with either lacquer or paint thinner. By employing a thinner, color and grain show up temporarily in clear relief while the grain is neither raised nor discolored.

Open and Closed Grain

As a tree grows the wood fibers naturally run in a longitudinal direction. In some species there is greater distance between fibers, and the resulting lumber is called open-grained. Woods such as oak, ash, and walnut are open-grained, and no matter how much sanding takes place, there will always be this minute unevenness through the finished surface. Wood fillers can be used to even the grain but the pronounced pattern will always be there. Close-grained woods such as maple, cherry, and beech will not bend as well, but will take a smoother polish.

Grading Lumber

The federal government has established standards for grading both hardwood and softwood. A softwood species such as pine is graded according to the following continuum (it comes in random widths and lengths unless specified):

#4 common	poor grade, unsuitable for fine furniture
#3 common #2 common	good for secondary wood
#1 shop grade	small knots but considerable clarity
"D" selects	quite clear, serviceable for most uses
"C" selects and better	virtually free of knots and imperfections

Hardwoods follow a different scale. Walnut, for example, is graded as follows:

#2 common	considerable sapwood, knots, narrow widths and short lengths
#1 common	clear sections within a board but quite spotty
Selects and better	considerable clear sections, nearly all usable, a good general grade
Factory and shop grade	virtually clear, good widths and lengths

The criteria for determining into which classification a board falls are complex, and include factors such as width, length, knots, splits or cracks, color, and percentage of clear grain.

Other Shop Materials

While lumber is the primary material, a wide range of other materials is needed to build furniture in the Shaker style. This includes glue. The Shakers, along with other builders of cabinetry in the nineteenth century, were limited to either hide glue or fish glue. While these glues are extremely effective in bonding wood, their application is messy, time-consuming, and odorous. If you have ever smelled a drop of hide glue on an electric hot plate, you have endured the unendurable. Fortunately, modern chemistry has carried us a long way from the days of the old glue pot. Probably the most widely used general cabinet adhesive is white glue. It provides an excellent bond, especially if the glued pieces are clamped under pressure. It sets in half an hour on softwoods and forty-five minutes on hardwoods. If the room temperature falls below 60°F., however, the glue turns chalky and loses its bonding properties. An aliphatic resin glue, a light yellow in color, can be used in temperatures as low as 45°F. It sets in half the time of white glue and has, it is claimed, twice the strength. Both types are used in our shop, white glue when slower drying is required, as in

PULLS & KNOBS

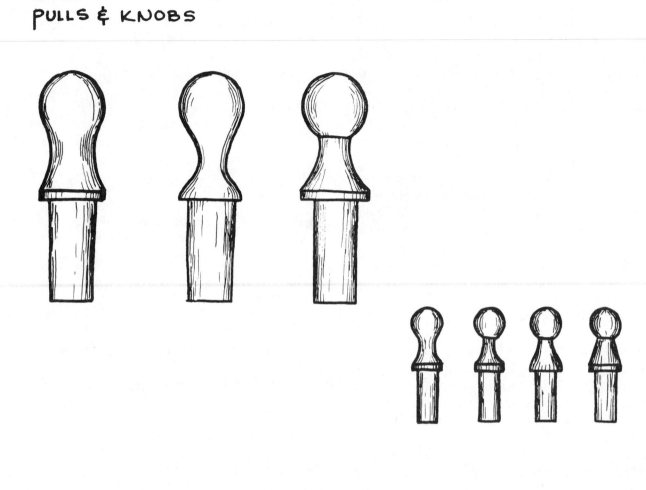

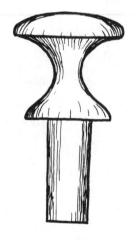

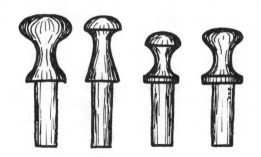

COATED ABRASIVES				
Very Fine	Fine	Medium	Coarse	Very Coarse
400 (10/0)	180 (5/0)	100 (2/0)	50 (1)	30 (2½)
280 (8/0)	150 (4/0)	80 (1/0)	40 (1½)	24 (3)
220 (6/0)	120 (3/0)	60 (1/2)	36 (2)	20 (3½)

gluing complicated dovetail joints, and yellow glue for quicker drying. With proper clamping and surface preparation, there really is no need for the countless other glue products on the market. Except for the occasional use of contact cement on clock faces or for veneer work, we use no other glue products.

Abrasives

More time is spent in sanding than in any other phase of the woodworking operation. Familiarity with a wide range of abrasives is necessary to achieve efficiency. Sandpaper is graded according to coarseness (size of grit particles), the distance between particles (open coat having greater open spaces than closed coat), and the substance of

abrasive particles (aluminum oxide, garnet carborundum, or silicon carbide). When working in softwood, particularly white pine with its abundance of pitch, open coat is slower to gum and therefore to be desired. For hardwood, closed coat paper lasts longer and does a better job. Hand sanding is performed using 9-inch by 11-inch sheets of production paper covered with silicon carbide. These can be cut and folded to fit hand-sanding blocks of various sorts.

Coarseness is categorized according to grit number; the lower the number, the coarser the paper. For most heavy sanding a rough grade of 40 will cut quickly into the wood's surface, 60 and 80 grits are good for soft shaping and leveling, while 120 gives a basically smooth finish suitable for paint. If the wood is to be polished, 220 grit will provide a satin smooth finish ready for oil or

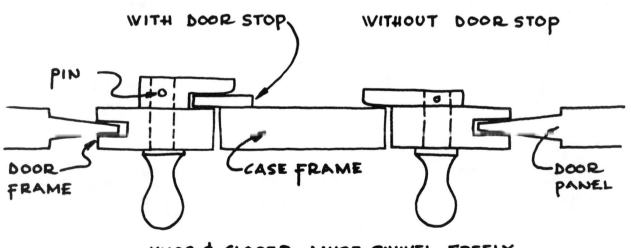

DOOR CLOSERS

WITH DOOR STOP   WITHOUT DOOR STOP

PIN

DOOR FRAME   CASE FRAME   DOOR PANEL

KNOB & CLOSER MUST SWIVEL FREELY

varnish. Once oil, varnish, or paint is applied, sanding with 220 or even 400 will provide that smooth, deep finish found only on hand-rubbed surfaces.

Power sanders, be they belt, oscillating, or disc type, use paper which is graded in the same way. We use aluminum oxide papers in our belt sanders because they seem to last longer. As a rule, once 120 grit paper has been used in a sanding machine, the finer grits are applied with production paper using a hand-sanding block. In any case, a full range of paper should also be on hand.

Hardware

There are hundreds of types of nails used in home and industry. The two of general interest to the cabinetmaker are common nails (nails having flat, disc-shaped heads) and finish nails (having the smallest head possible). Both types are graded according to wire thickness and length. For example, a 4d (fourpenny) nail is 1½″ long, an 8d (eightpenny) is 2½″ long and a 10d (tenpenny) is 3¼″ long. The longer the nail, the heavier the gauge of the wire, of course. Therefore, 4d common nails number 300 to the pound, and 16d number 45.

Common

Finish

Common nails are used in only the crudest work and would never be found in fine cabinetry. Indeed, with a very few exceptions, finish nails should not be used in cabinetry at all. In our shop, an occasional 4d finish nail is used to fasten a cupboard back or drawer glide but never to fasten a joint. Occasionally, mouldings might be fastened with finishing nails, but for most practical purposes, both common and finishing nails should be relegated to making jigs and crates and cleaning fingernails.

As a designer, I've tried to create furniture using exclusively wooden joints and fasteners. In the plans contained here, you will see that mortise and tenon is used instead of bolt and nut—that splined miter joints are used rather than corrugated fasteners. However, in spite of our good efforts, there remain a number of joint problems that can best be solved by use of a screw.

No cabinet shop is complete without an inventory of screws. Since there is such an enormous array of sizes, combinations of length and wire (diameter), it is wise to adopt a standard system of inventory. This will standardize drill sizes,

MAKING A BUTTERFLY HINGE:

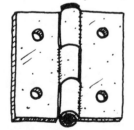

START WITH STEEL HINGE. GRIND OFF PIN BOTTOM. REMOVE PIN.

GRIND, FILE OR SAW HINGE INTO BUTTER-FLY SHAPE. CUT PIN TO LENGTH AND RE-INSERT.

THISTLE END

HAMMER EDGES AND WINGS. BLUE WITH TORCH, OR PLACE IN WOOD STOVE.

HINGES

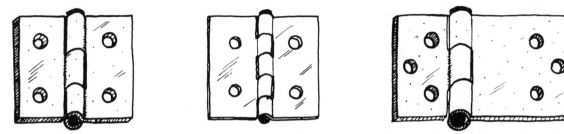

STEEL   BRASS   STEEL DROP-LEAF

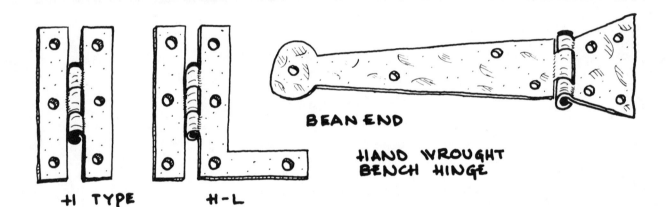

H TYPE   H-L

BEAN END

HAND WROUGHT
BENCH HINGE

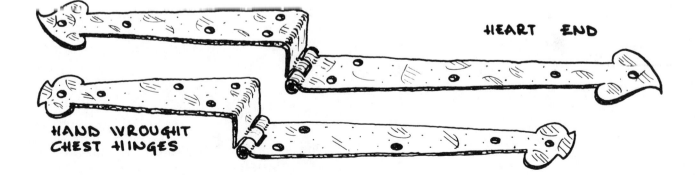

HEART END

HAND WROUGHT
CHEST HINGES

countersink sizes, screwdriver sizes, and pung or plug sizes. A small assortment of brass flathead screws should be on hand for mounting hinges and should be matched to the hinge to be used. The following sizes of steel screws should be on hand for these suggested applications:

Length	Gauge	Typical Use
⅝″	#10	Table hinges
¾″	#4	Fine fastenings—rarely used but good to have
1¼″	#8	General use, most widely used in joining ¾″ lumber
1½″	#8	Slightly heavier applications, mounting tabletop to base, etc.
2″	#10	Joining ¾″ member to 1¾″ member
3″	#16	Extremely heavy use—rarely used but needed

By confining the bulk of screw sizes to #8 gauge, a standard drill bit can be fitted with a ⅜-inch countersink, reducing many steps in what would otherwise become a confusing process. In addition to this array of flathead screws, an assortment of oval head, blue roundhead, and other specialty screws is good to have on hand.

Dowels

Along with this screw assortment should be a collection of select northern hardwood dowel sizes. Useful in making pins for pegging mortise and tenon joints, end grain plugs for covering screw holes, hinge pins, etc., dowels are indispensable. An assortment consisting of ⅛″, ¼″, ⅜″, ½″, ⅝″ and ¾″ should be on hand. Buy these in 36-inch, 42-inch, or 48-inch lengths—they are cheaper and can always be cut into shorter lengths later.

Additional dowels can be made on a drill press using a dowel cutter. The advantage here is that one can make a dowel out of any wood, and the dowel end can be crossdgrained, producing an "invisible" plug.

Pulls and Knobs

One of the characteristics which so distinguished early nineteenth-century Shaker furniture was the refinement of door and drawer pulls. While contemporaries were applying ornate brass, porcelain, and even pressed-glass drawer pulls, the early nineteenth-century Shakers maintained the simple turned wooden pull in almost all of their work. This graceful knob, along with the turned wooden hanging peg set in horizontal rows, has been the hallmark of Shaker understatement and utility. In order to build this genre of furniture one should have access to a wood lathe where these can be turned in an unlimited variety.

Hinges

Cast-iron butt hinges were developed in the late 1700s and were used in most early Shaker case work. They were always countersunk into stiles and were hand-dsome and durable. Prior to this, hinges were wrought by hand and, because of the unevenness of their surfaces and inconstancy of size, were usually shaped in the form of H, HL, strap, or butterfly and surface mounted. They were secured either with oval screws or with clinched, wrought nails. Wrought and cast hinges are no longer commonly available. When a flush-mounted wrought hinge is required in our work, we either commission a local blacksmith to fashion it or we re-work (distress, the term in the antique business) ordinary steel butt hinges. These are re-shaped on an anvil, the edges are sm-oothed with either a file or bench grinder and then "blued" by heating them with a butane torch. When applying these, or wrought hardware of any kind, oval or round head blue screws should be used. If these are not available, ordinary steel screws will work, but they also must be blued with the torch. Most screws today are offered with a zinc plating which has to be ground or filed off before coloring.

When butt hinges are required, we use solid brass. Neither stamped raw steel nor brass-plated steel will do. The leaves of the hinges should fit the thickness of the door. If, for example, the door thickness and case stile are ¾", then a ⅝" or ¾" hinge leaf is correct. Naturally, these are mounted with brass screws, and the whole is burnished after being attached to the case.

The Quality of Materials

In purchasing shop supplies, particularly those items that go directly into the shop's product, every effort should be made to use only the very best. Since labor represents three quarters of the cost of production, it seems to me to be a fundamental absurdity to try to cut corners by using cheap materials. It simply doesn't pay. Excellence is achieved only through the use of superior raw materials.

Chapter 3

Tools

The Nature of Workmanship

In discussing the merits of a particular piece of furniture one often hears that it is handmade. To some, handmade equates with clumsy or crude. My first helper in the shop had a strong notion of what was expected of a handmade piece. His work was scarred with plough plane marks, rough end grain left from the pull of a draw knife, and hammer tracks everywhere. To him, handmade meant tool marks—the more tools marks the more handmade. This notion that handmade means rustic is a little upsetting, and is not confined to wood products. How often have you heard that an oriental rug is more desirable when it exhibits design mistakes and abrupt color changes. Persians, who know better, say that such defective workmanship is the result of inexperience or dullness of mind and good only for export to the European and American markets where it is lauded as proof positive of "hand-madeness" or antiquity. Somehow there is the notion that if the work of a given craftsman is too perfect in finish and detail it will be confused with machine-made and therefore be of less value. Accordingly, some craftsmen purposely "distress" their work, not to give it instant age, but to mark it "handmade" for all to plainly see.

America's current infatuation with that which is handmade is a relatively recent phenomenon. As a youngster I can remember our total commitment to the miracle of the machine. A 1930 book on machine wood tools says, "With the use of power-driven machines, articles of wood may be made as attractive and as well constructed as any factory-made product." To most of us in crafts today this sentiment is roughly inside out: hand tools achieve the ultimate attractiveness. At another point the author states, "The ring of the whirling circular saw or the hum of the jointer is music to the ears of any real man or boy. . . ." What would the feminists and OSHA have to say about this? And so to some, handmade means crude, primitive and cheap while to others machine-made means slick, lifeless and cheap. Is this a clash of taste, a confrontation of values? Probably not. The whole issue of handmade versus machine-made is clouded by sloppy terminology.

Strictly speaking, the only handmade object, so far as I know, is free-formed clay pottery which is sun dried. No tools are used, just the fingers and nature's processes. However, we use the term "handmade" more loosely and apply it to processes that include the use of tools of every sort. And this, of course, is why the term really isn't very serviceable. A better distinction, certainly a more interesting one, was advanced some years ago by a British philosopher who, when discussing the nature of workmanship, used the terms "manufacture of risk" and "manufacture of non-risk." According to this dichotomy, what separates one class of goods from another isn't the use of hands but rather the risk that was present during the manufacturing process. In other words, a man working slowly in a shop, utilizing both powered and nonpowered tools but without elaborate jigs, templates, and automatic clamping devices, runs the risk of making a mistake at almost every turn. As he proceeds, step by step, a multitude of variables affect the outcome of his efforts. He never really knows how it will look when he finishes. And if he makes more than one, the parts will probably not be interchangeable, and certainly the finished objects will all be different.

The manufacture of non-risk, too, may or may not use power-driven tools and human hands, but because elaborate steps are taken at replicating parts with extremely close tolerances, the outcome of the manufacturing process is guaranteed at the very beginning. There is no risk: the outcome is predetermined and has been programmed into the manufacturing process.

Hence, as our philosopher advises, man soon becomes bored looking at a parking lot full of shiny new cars, manufactured with no risk as to outcome, one indistinguishable from another. Yet take the same man to a fishing harbor crowded with small boats of every description and he will spend hours delighting at the differences before him. Is it fair to say the boats, because each one is designed and crafted one at a time, are better built than the cars? I think not. Rather, the manufacture of risk is a far more humane enterprise for both the builder and the perceiver. The human eye thrives on differences, the mind on the unexpected, and the soul on the individuality of human production.

Therefore, in discussing tools let us see the tool not only as the extension of the human hand but as the extension of the spirit as well. In our shop we use power tools, jigs, templates of various sorts, and so on, but we control them, they do not control us.

I have an acquaintance who builds Windsor chairs for a living in Portsmouth, New Hampshire, in the original way. He uses no power equipment except the electric light bulb for illumination and a one-third horsepower motor to drive the lathe. I used to argue that he could increase production by using a bandsaw and a pneumatic sander, but to no avail. Now, three years later, he is still producing two chairs a week and has a sixteen-month backlog of orders.

Several months ago we built in our shop a run of about fifty Windsor chairs, one at a time, of course, but we used all the tools available to us—and each of us produced an average of ten chairs a week.

Which of us is right? Neither, and both. What distinguishes us is not our product but our process. One wishes to relive a bygone era by committing himself to the exacting methods of the past, where the *process* is as important as, indeed more important than, the *product*. The other places product first and uses the most efficient method to create it. The danger to the former is that he may become an anachronism by feeding his ego while ignoring his stomach. The danger to the latter is that efficiency can become an iron mistress demanding more and more repetition, more and more volume, and, ultimately, interchangeability and diminishing quality control. The result is cataclysmic. The result is mass production, the manufacture of non-risk, where furniture is designed not because of aesthetic imperatives but because this curve or that profile happens to fit the machine. The Shakers worked both ways. They used both hand tools and power tools and in most of their early work built one at a time following the manufacture of risk. However, by 1870 they mass-produced chairs which had a national distribution. Although well-built, the later, mass-produced furniture lacks the spontaneity of their earlier work.

In producing, we have made a number of concessions to the twentieth century, yet we firmly hold to the axiom that tools are the servants of man and not the masters. How many tools, and which ones, are needed to build a chest of drawers? As few or as many as you wish, depending on how much time you have and on how skillful you are. When my wife and I were married, I built a small house with only an electric sabre saw (jigsaw) and ten or fifteen hand tools. It took forever, but what a learning experience! In buying hand tools two generalizations are in order. If you are buying a new tool, always buy the best quality available. Nothing is quite so counterproductive as cheap tools that aren't balanced, don't hold a sharp edge, or can't be sharpened at all. Second, when a choice exists between a new tool and one, say, a hundred years old, I'll opt for the old one every time. The steel used today simply doesn't seem to compare. I have both new and old tools and somehow the hand almost always reaches for the antique. To some extent this is also true of heavier power equipment, but more on that later.

Hand Saws

Rip Saw: Having rather large, steeply cut teeth, four and one-half to the inch, with some "set" (teeth alternatively bent outward), the rip saw is used in cutting with the grain. Set in a saw allows the teeth to cut a slot (kerf) slightly wider than the saw blade so the blade can pass without binding.

Crosscut Saw: Unlike the rip, the crosscut has teeth tapered both on the forward and trailing edges, seven to the inch, and is used for cutting diagonally or across the wood grain.

Both are operated by pushing and should never be forced or buckling is likely to occur, causing a permanent crimp in the blade. When sawing, use a steady rhythm, letting the weight of the saw cause the teeth to bite with each stroke. An occasional *light* coat of fine machine oil helps keep all saws clean.

Backsaw: Having a back rib for stiffness, the backsaw is a slightly thinner version of the crosscut; but much finer. For general purposes a backsaw with about fifteen teeth to the inch is satisfactory for a number of cutting jobs such as making tenons, miter cuts, and so on. The blade of a versatile backsaw should not be more than fourteen inches long.

Dovetail Saw: For all fine cutting, where a razor-thin cut with well defined edges is required, the best tool is the dovetail saw. This is essentially a thin backsaw with from twenty-two to twenty-six teeth per inch. A full wooden handle is preferred, since it offers considerably more control than the simple turned handle. To achieve a close tolerance when cutting with a dovetail saw, a very sharp pencil or, better, a thin scribe mark is useful. By scribing along the cut before the cut is made one can almost fence the saw and achieve a

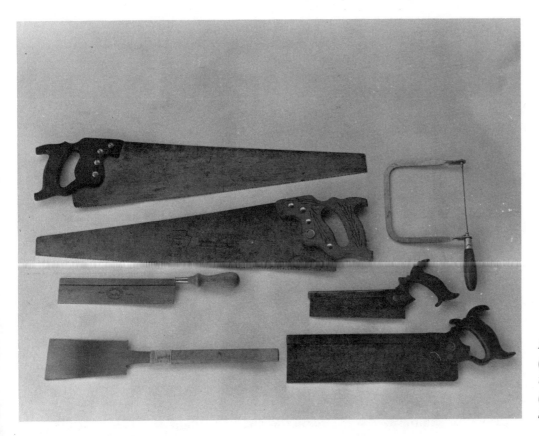

From top to bottom: (left) rip, crosscut, dovetail, Japanese crosscut; (right) coping, original Shaker dovetail, backsaw.

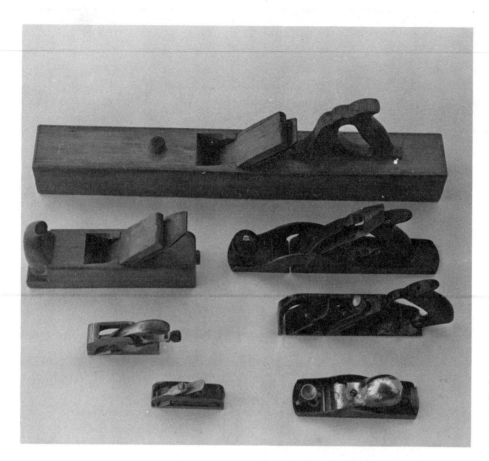

The large wooden plane is a jointer; smaller one is a jack plane. The steel planes are (largest to smallest) rabbet, rabbet with fence, block, and two small rabbet planes.

near perfect cut.

Coping Saw: Sometimes called a hand jigsaw, the coping saw consists of a frame with adjustable blades which vary in coarseness, depending on the nature of the work. This is a useful tool for circulinear cutting and for cutting inside holes; but it is not recommended for cutting straight lines.

Japanese Saw: For unknown reasons the handsaw in the western world evolved as a pushing instrument, whereas in Asia saws are pulled through the cutting stroke. This permits the use of a much thinner blade with no rib since buckling is not encountered. These saws are unsurpassed for flush-cutting any protrusion, particularly dowels.

Planes

Jointer Plane: Also called the tryplane, the jointer plane is used in preparing an edge for gluing to another edge. In order to achieve straightness the plane is over twenty inches long, and when properly sharpened and adjusted, it is capable of creating a totally flat, straight edge.

Jack Plane: Good for general use, the jack plane is a must for the carpenter who hangs doors and windows and fits paneling. This tool is similar to the jointer plane, but is only fourteen or fifteen inches long.

Block Plane: While only six inches long, this is a surfacing, trimming, and edging plane of limitless use. Although harder to keep adjusted than the larger planes, it is, in my experience, one of the most necessary planes in the shop.

Rabbet Plane: Although they come in a variety of sizes and styles, all rabbet planes share the capacity to cut clean, squared channels along edges. For general purpose rabbeting elaborate fencing systems are not necessary.

Moulding Planes: Traditionally made of wood

MOULDING KNIFE HEAD PROFILES

DADO

OGEE

BEAD

TONGUE

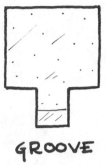

GROOVE

QUARTER
COVE
TABLE LEAF

THUMB NOSE
TABLE TOP

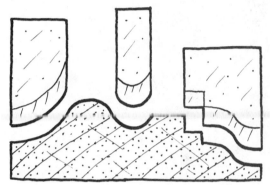

THREE MOULDING PLANES
APPLIED TO COMPOUND
PROFILE.

A collection of moulding planes. While most are made of beech, the fancy fillister is built of brass, steel, apple, and rosewood.

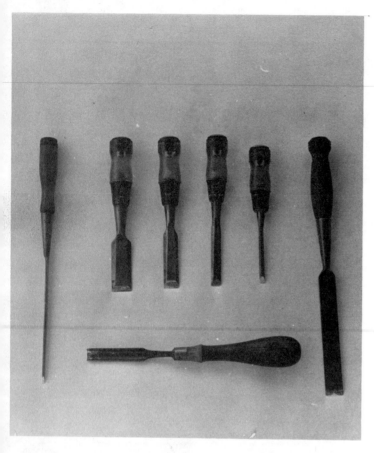

*From left: 1/8" mortise chisel; 1", 3/4", 1/2",
and 1/4" bevel chisels; and 3/4" long-blade
mortise chisel. At bottom is 3/8" gouge.*

Brace and eggbeater.

with a primitive adjusting wedge, moulding planes were made to hold an almost endless assortment of knives to cut everything from a simple dado to the most elaborate bolection mouldings of an earlier time. I have over fifty, and no two are alike. Sometimes moulding planes come in sets for use in cutting tongue-and-groove or matched-edge mouldings for drop-leaf tables. The router, the table saw moulding head, and the spindle shaper have made most of these old planes obsolete, yet they are themselves works of art worth treasuring.

Chisels

Although literally hundreds of chisel shapes exist, all fall roughly into three categories: *firmer*, *bevel*, and *gouge*. In addition to this variety of blade shapes there are numerous types of handles, both wooden and synthetic fiber.

The *firmer* is the basic chisel pattern. It offers durability and has a flat side which helps in aligning the tool for square cuts. The *bevel* chisel has a little greater flexibility than the firmer since it can get in and out of closer quarters, as in dovetail slots. Since virtually all modern chisels are now beveled, this distinction is somewhat academic. Because chisels are both struck with a mallet and pushed by hand, it is wise to buy them with plastic handles that will withstand rough treatment. Although I have dozens of chisels, I find that 99 percent of my work can be accomplished with ⅛'' and ½'' firmers, and a ¼'', ½'', ¾'' and 1'' standard bevel set. For special dovetail work I use a ⅜'' and ⅝'' bevel which allows one-stroke cutting. I also have a ¾'' x 8'' chisel which gives a longer reach before hitting the hilt of the handle and a ¾'' x 2'' stubby chisel for close-in work, such as inside assembled cases.

Gouges come in hundreds of shapes and sizes. While this variety is useful to the wood carver, it is quite unnecessary for the cabinetmaker. One or two, say a ⅜'' and a ¾'', are enough to handle most problems associated with cabinetry.

The angle of a chisel tip should be about 30°. Your own experience will dictate whether you want to drop that down to 25° or increase it to

From left: rattail rasp, half-round rasp, bastard file, half-round file, rattail file.

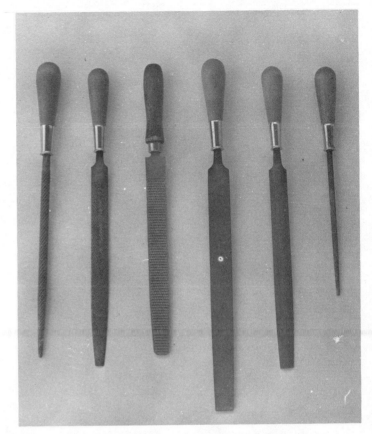

35°. In any case, the tip should be slightly hollow ground and well sharpened.

Of all the tools in the shop the lowly chisel has extracted the most blood from my veins! The meaty part of my left hand is a mass of scars from at least six separate cuts, ranging in severity from just over superficial to bone-deep. Moral of the story: (1) never hold wood in one hand and push the chisel with the other, and (2) always work with the chisel moving away from any part of your body. Remember, a properly sharpened chisel is a razor blade without the safety head. Treat it with respect.

From left: auger bit, flat bit, wood-boring twist bit, metal-boring twist bit, expansion bit, Forstner bit, countersink, tapered twist with countersink, screwdriver bit, plug cutter.

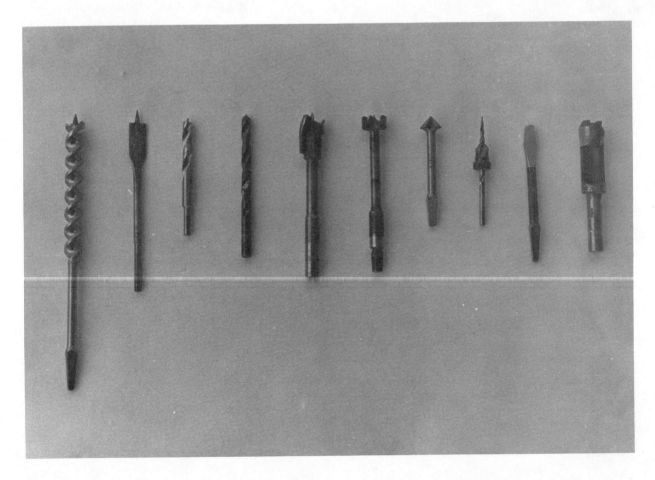

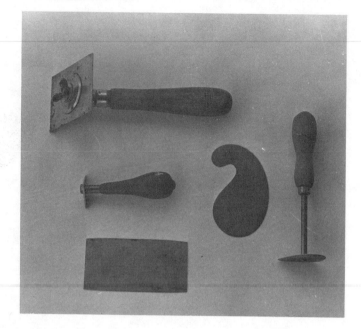

At left: assorted scrapers.

Drills

Large wood-boring bits are turned with the *brace* while smaller twist drill bits, say $1/16''$ to $3/8''$, are turned in an *eggbeater* drill. Braces come equipped with a two-jaw chuck which receives both round- and square-shanked drill bits; however, the round shanks tend to twist in the chuck under pressure. The brace can also be used effectively as a means of achieving greater torque in driving screws. Again, the portable power drill has largely replaced the hand drill for almost all operations. However, when accuracy is sought, the slowness of the hand drill makes it superior to its electric counterpart.

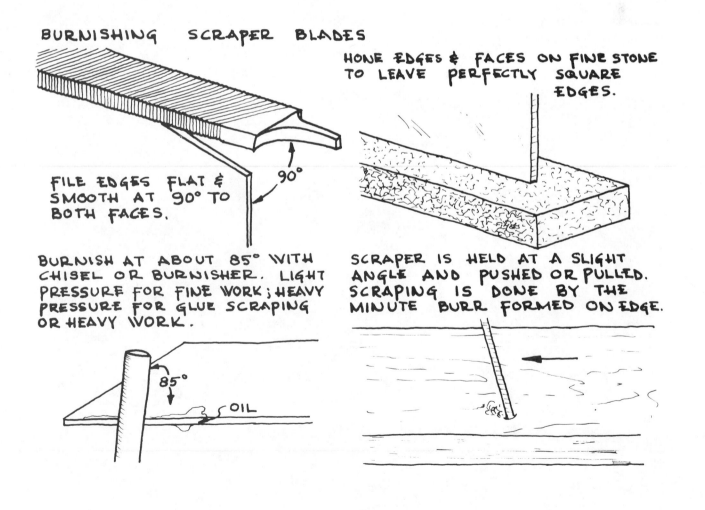

BURNISHING SCRAPER BLADES

FILE EDGES FLAT & SMOOTH AT 90° TO BOTH FACES.

90°

HONE EDGES & FACES ON FINE STONE TO LEAVE PERFECTLY SQUARE EDGES.

BURNISH AT ABOUT 85° WITH CHISEL OR BURNISHER. LIGHT PRESSURE FOR FINE WORK; HEAVY PRESSURE FOR GLUE SCRAPING OR HEAVY WORK.

85°

OIL

SCRAPER IS HELD AT A SLIGHT ANGLE AND PUSHED OR PULLED. SCRAPING IS DONE BY THE MINUTE BURR FORMED ON EDGE.

Draw knife.

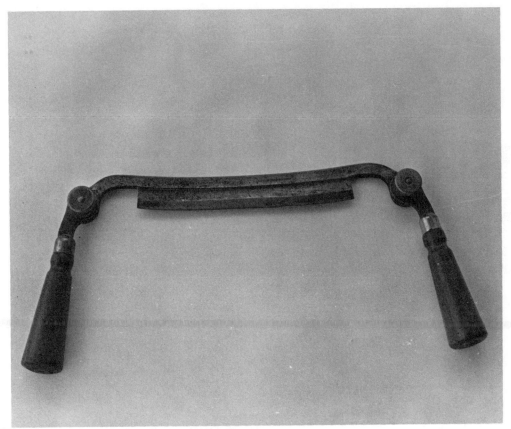

Drill Bits

The common *auger bit* is generally the most useful bit in the brace. Borings of ¼″ to 2″ can be achieved with a good set of augers. In making larger borings, the *expansion bit* is indispensable. Its great advantage derives from its ability to cut any diameter one wishes. The *Forstner bit* performs the job of the auger, but offers the advantage of exceptionally clean walls and a flat bottom to the hole. It is an excellent bit for use in cutting plug holes over unwanted knots and is also used in boring the holes into which the nuts are placed in bed and table construction. Here, an auger tip would cut too deep.

    Twist bits are of two types, wood boring and

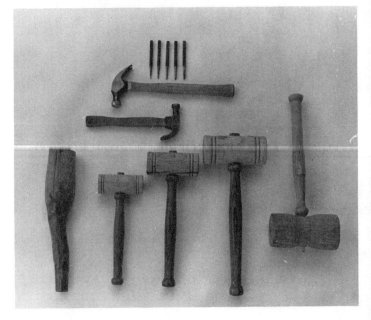

At right: a set of nail sets, 12-ounce hammer, 6-ounce hammer, assorted mallets.

Above: C-clamps, bar clamps, and clamping rack.

Below: bar clamps.

metal boring. By far the most common and useful bit in the shop is the metal cutting version. It is recommended that a set of from eight to twelve, ranging in diameter from $1/16$'' to $1/2$'', be on hand at all times. Some woodworkers prefer to re-grind the tips of their twist bits, elongating the taper. This leaves a cleaner hole.

Flat bits, sometimes called butterfly bits, are excellent for use in high-speed drills but should not be used in either the eggbeater or the brace. The advantage of the flat bit over the twist bit is cost and ease of sharpening. Never buy two-piece flat bits since they break easily with continual use.

Countersinks are useful when boring holes to receive screw heads. Another useful bit is the *tapered twist bit with countersink* attached. The cheaper types of flat drills with self-countersinking flanges simply don't hold up. If screw sizes are standardized, then two or three of these combinations are sufficient.

The *plug cutter*, which can be used with the brace, electric drill, or drill press, is handy in making dowels and plugs either through side grain or end grain. Several sizes, perhaps $3/8$'' and $1/2$'', are useful. Remember, match this diameter to the countersink size mentioned above for use in making plugs to cover screw heads. Again, the need for standardizing screw sizes is imperative.

Rasps and Files

Rasps are coarse files with triangular shaped teeth which cut quickly. Rasps are used in rough shaping, while standard files are good for finish work. Half-round and round rasps and files are useful and should always be on hand. The rasp should be coarse, and the file of moderate coarseness. A wire file card should be used after a file has seen sustained use. A dirty file or a dull file is a worthless instrument. If a file becomes dull, it can be sharpened by placing it outdoors on the grass to absorb the early morning dew. I don't know what happens but it seems to work. This only works once or twice, and after that the file should be replaced. Don't throw away old files, since they

At left: a set of six cabinetmaker's screwdrivers, Phillips screwdriver, and steel screwdriver.

At right: large wooden square, steel square, set of four try squares, sliding miter square, bevel square.

make excellent chisels, knives, and moulding plane blades. One of the men in our shop has built a complete set of carving tools and lathe tools from discarded files. When grinding them, however, care must be taken not to overheat them and thereby draw their temper.

Draw Knife

For quick, coarse shaping nothing equals the draw knife. The experience of shaping with both hands separated by a sharp shaft of steel must be experienced to be understood. It is quite difficult to master, but once learned becomes a natural extension of the hands, arms, and shoulders. A dull draw knife is an abomination. If you can't shave with it, don't use it!

Scrapers

A simple flat piece of steel properly sharpened is indispensable in the shop. Scrapers can be made with or without handles in any shape desired. A number of scrapers are on the market and all of them work if kept sharp. This is achieved through grinding and then burnishing, which puts a slight burr on the edge. A properly ground and shaped scraper can do wondrous things.

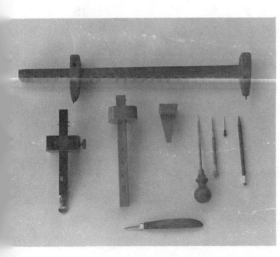

At left: Two scribing gauges at left, and assorted tools for scribing sharp lines.

At right: mechanical and home-made miter boxes.

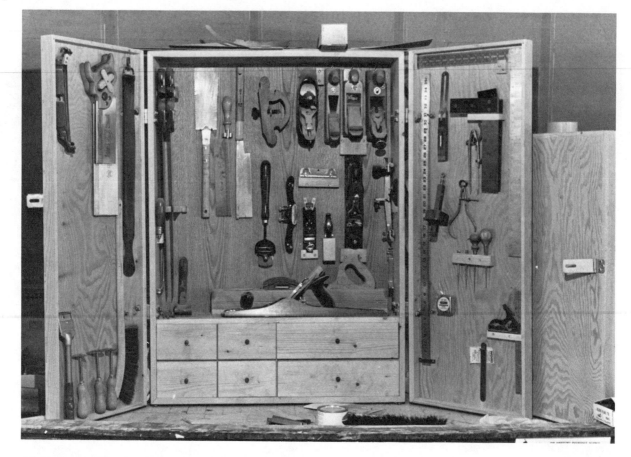

If Chris doesn't have it in one of these boxes, it either doesn't exist or it can't be used.

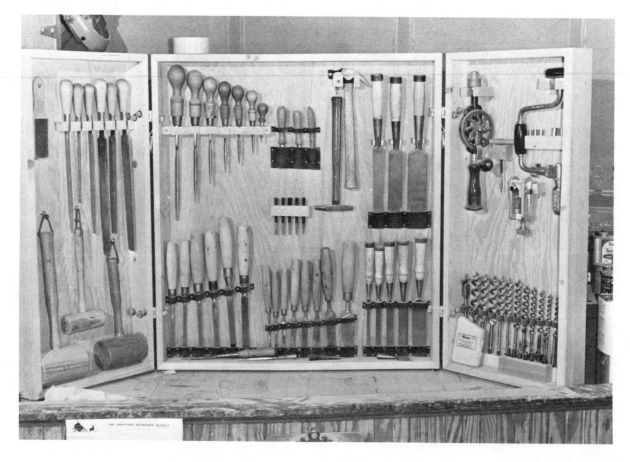

Hammers and Mallets

A ten- to twelve-ounce hammer is sufficiently heavy for almost all cabinetry needs. A lighter one, four to six ounces, is good to have for driving fine brads. A hammer should not be used in driving a wood chisel since the steel head will eventually wreck the chisel. For this a wooden mallet, fashioned in beech, ash, lignum vitae, apple, or some other hardwood is used. I'm not sure it matters what type of mallet is used as long as there are two or three sizes for different degrees of impact. One type of mallet works as well as any other, it simply depends on what one becomes used to. In our shop one man uses only a light ash cylindrical mallet he made as a boy, another uses a conical shaped affair he turned in lignum vitae, still another uses a crude club fashioned from the branch of an apple tree. I use a simple plastic mallet for which I paid $1.25.

Clamps

Bar clamps provide pressure when gluing up panels and carcass assemblies; without them few sizable objects can be made. Several types are manufactured which adapt to steel water pipe. These bend, twist, and jam and shouldn't be purchased. Only the bar type seems suitable for a full range of uses. A minimum set of four 24-inch, four 48-inch, and four 72-inch clamps would be advisable in a modestly equipped shop. Hard rubber covers can be obtained to slip over the pressure plates and protect semifinished wood assemblies. It is also advisable to build a clamping rack or table with slots cut at equal intervals. By setting the bar clamps on a flat surface it is easier to glue up a flat panel.

For smaller clamping jobs the simple C-clamp is used. A good starting set might be two six-inch, two eight-inch, and two twelve-inch. Often these are used in conjunction with small softwood blocks which protect product surfaces. In addition to these, a small assortment of wooden handscrew clamps is useful. Again, two or three sizes are desirable.

Beyond these, there exist dozens of other types of clamping devices. The three aforementioned all

Above: portable circular saw.

Below: portable sabre or jig saw.

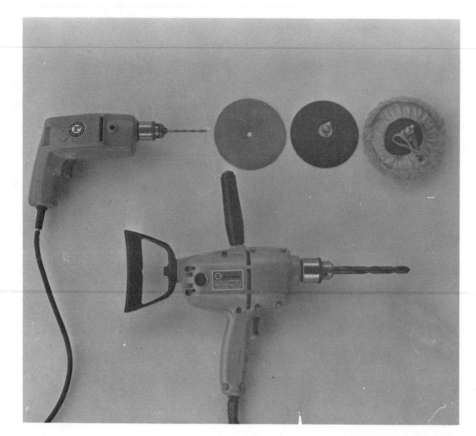

A 3/8" drill and a 1/2" drill with disc attachments. Both drills are variable speed.

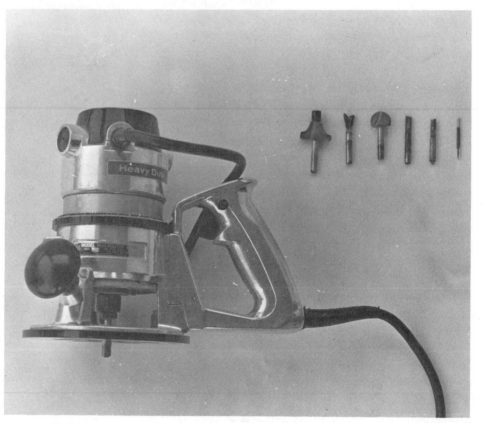

Router.

use the threaded screw for pressure. There are, in addition, incline wedges which can be driven into various frames and onto the work bench itself. There is the rope tourniquet, which works particularly well on chairs and mitered mirror and picture frames. Clamps seem to be the most ignored tool in the shop. They are out of mind until needed, and then they're usually not to be found. Without a good set of clamps the cabinetmaker is handicapped considerably.

Screwdrivers

Although any good set of screwdrivers will suffice, I like the cabinetmaker's screwdrivers made in England and sold in many specialty supply shops. They fit the hand and provide an excellent grip. In addition to a set of five or seven of these, an old-fashioned wood and steel handled screwdriver is great for rough work, and you can use a mallet on it. Several Phillips head screwdrivers will also be necessary for working on power tools and installing some prepackaged hardware. All screwdriver blades should be kept with sharp corners and trim to avoid chewing up screw heads.

Squares

In squaring case pieces and relatively long right-angle cuts the *steel square*, or carpenter's square, is an excellent tool. To the knowledgeable it can be used in determining angles, both simple and compound. In fact, this square is so versatile in house construction, for example, that our local vocational school offers a complete course on the use of the steel square. For even larger squaring, a square built of wood can be useful. If a large framing square is built, it should be checked for accuracy every now and then, since it will tend to "give" with use.

A more useful tool for marking as well as measuring is the *try square*, which comes in graduated sizes, two or three of which, from four inches to ten inches, are handiest. An improvement is the *sliding miter try square*, which can be used as a 90° square, a 45° miter gauge, a depth gauge, a steel straight edge, a ruler, and a marking

gauge. Being adjustable, the *bevel square* can be set at any angle; it is useful in scribing dovetails and other angles.

Scribing Gauge

The scribing gauge is indispensable for marking out joints such as dovetail, rabbet, dado, and miter. The scribing pin itself should be kept sharp, and the distance to the hilt should always be checked with a rule.

Miter Box

For occasional hand-cutting of miter joints using a backsaw or dovetail saw, a simple three-sided wooden box, built in a close-grained hardwood and fitted with accurately placed kerfs, is adequate. For more accuracy and greater longevity a more elaborate miter saw is available and useful.

There are, in addition to this basic list of hand tools, literally hundreds of other gadgets sold in hardware stores and specialty houses throughout the country. In my experience, most of these so-called labor-saving devices are rather worthless contraptions which appeal to man's propensity for collecting things rather than to rational judgment. I'm sure the same is true in the kitchen, where a "revolutionary device" is introduced every four hours and demonstrated in department stores and on late-night television. This is not to suggest that other handtools are not useful to the artisan. Let us simply conclude by saying that a mastery of these basic tools should precede other more technical or exotic contrivances.

Portable Power Tools

Circular saw: The portable power handsaw was introduced as a tool for carpenters who build houses. In this capacity it has limitless potential; in the cabinet shop one can get by without such a tool. Still, we use it for cutting dados in the sides of large case pieces, for cutting tenons on table tops when breadboarding, and for trimming off overhanging secondary wood. The most common

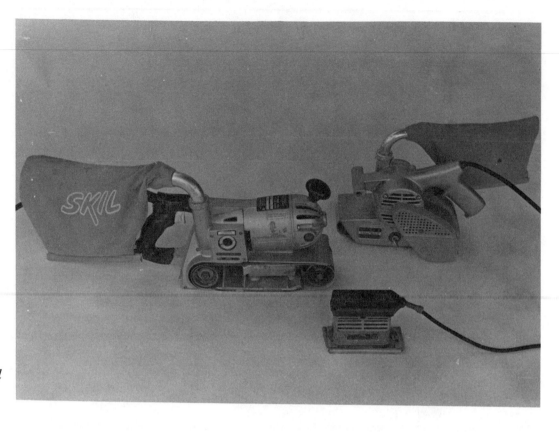

*Belt sanders and
small orbital
sander.*

size takes a 7½ inch blade, for which a variety of blades is made. For virtually all cabinet work a combination blade is recommended. For extremely fine work, which is difficult to manage with such a crude tool, a fine-toothed veneer blade is available. The best saws of this type are equipped with a large base plate which extends on *both sides* of the blade. This offers much greater support and allows the operator to cut from either side. Only the heavy-duty grade is worth buying, since the lighter ones, though much cheaper, tend to wear out field and armature windings and sleeve bearings quickly. What compounds this problem is the fact that these cheap tools cannot be easily repaired because the housings and bearings are integrated. It costs more to fix one than to buy a new one. This, of course, is true of all portable power equipment. Never buy the cheap ''handyman'' tools—they are no bargain. With practice, this tool is quite versatile. A close friend who has worked as a millwright and finish carpenter for over forty years can perform with this tool feats that are designed to astound and amaze. He can

even cut complete dovetails using only the portable circular saw.

Sabre Saw: Also called the portable jigsaw, this tool is a time-saver if the shop does not have a bandsaw. It is capable of fairly close scroll work and is excellent for cutting tabletop diameters and curved parts in wood up to two inches thick. With a little practice one can even start an inside cut without first boring a hole to admit the blade.

Power Drill: The portable power drill is a tool used daily for several operations. In boring holes the variable speed model affords greater flexibility and is capable of using both twist bits and flat bits. Because of its three-jaw chuck it cannot, of course, use the standard auger. When held to dead slow speed and if fitted with a screwdriver head, this tool is excellent for driving large numbers of screws. A seven-inch buffer kit can be fitted with a special sandpaper disc which will perform moderately well as a disc sander. When covered with a sheepskin pad, it becomes a buffer useful in polishing finished furniture. In purchasing a power drill, a ⅜-inch capacity, heavy-duty type is recommended. For extremely heavy boring and screwing, where greater torque is required, the ½-inch capacity is best. The small ¼-inch variety is so limited in its scope that it is not recommended for the serious woodworker.

Router: Running at over 3600 r.p.m., the router is capable of cutting a great variety of mouldings and interesting profiles. The enormous assortment of cutting heads and factory-made jigs provides a great range of possibilities, including fluting, beading, chamfering, rabbeting, dadoing, inletting hinges, and dovetailing. In short, this tool has effectively replaced that collection of moulding planes we discussed earlier. Where a spindle shaper is not available, the router is a good tool to have. Again the heavier the better, and the greater the plate surface the more stable the machine. A good router should be designed so that the operator can see clearly the cutting head

as it is working and so that he can change heads without a degree in engineering. My router affords neither of these advantages.

Sanders: Of all the tools in our shop the portable belt sander, by universal agreement, is singularly the most used and the most important. Without this labor saver there is no doubt we could not sell our furniture at a profit and compete with large manufacturers. It is used for *all* intermediate and final surface preparation and saves hundreds of hours weekly in leveling and smoothing all flat components. Where the joiner of yesterday hand-planed each member to fairly exacting dimensions before assembly, we work with rougher exterior surfaces and smooth only after the final assembly is completed. A man versed in the use of the sander can perform operations undreamed of by workers a generation ago, as long as he follows the grain of the wood and doesn't try to rush. Because of the volume of our work we burn out a belt sander every four or five

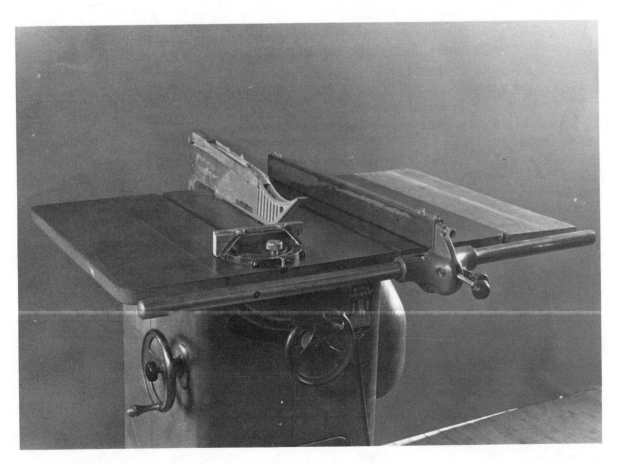

Ten-inch table saw.

months. We have used four different brands. We've learned from experience that the chain-driven, heavy-duty, self-lubricating sander is the most satisfactory, although it costs over twice as much as the common type. We use two sizes, 3″ x 21″ and 3″ x 24″, and we inventory 40, 60, 80 and 120 grit belts for both. If the surface is already fairly clean, the 60 grit, followed by the 120 grit, is adequate. The smaller sander has 2-inch rollers, the larger one has 2¼-inch rollers, and both can be used in grinding out concave shapes. To protect our lungs we equip our portable belt sanders with dust-collecting bags.

For fine sanding the orbital or pad sander is useful. Coarse grits should not be used with this machine since they leave telltale marks which are difficult to sand out. The small vibrator type does not perform well, since the longer the stroke or oscillation the better. Orbital sanders are only useful for final finishes.

Stationary Power Tools

Table Saw: The workhorse of any shop is the table saw. When mastered, it can save countless hours while achieving considerable accuracy. If a shop could have only one saw, it would be a ten-inch tilting arbor saw with a ⅝-inch arbor, a three horsepower double-belt-driven motor which develops a 4000-r.p.m. blade speed. The top would be milled cast steel and measure 28 inches

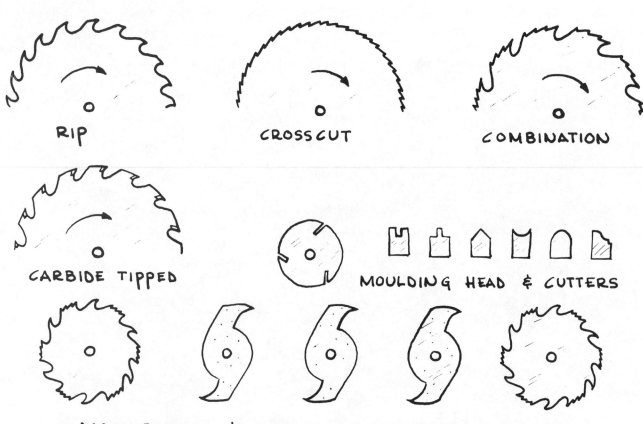

CIRCULAR SAW BLADES

RIP CROSSCUT COMBINATION

CARBIDE TIPPED MOULDING HEAD & CUTTERS

DADO BLADES & CHIPPERS OF VARIOUS THICKNESSES

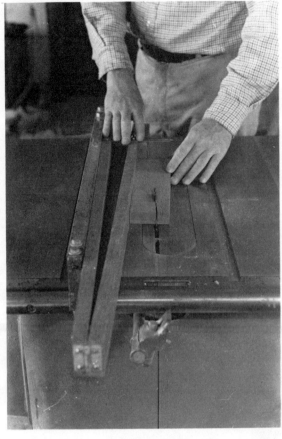

Top left: tenon jig attachment.

Left: finger spring forces stock to fence.

Above: adjustable tapering jig.

deep, 48 inches wide, and 34 inches high. It would have an adjustable insert to fit close to the blade. The parallel fence would have a combination front and rear locking handle at the front of the fence and would travel at least 25 inches from the blade on the extreme righthand side. The base would be completely enclosed to collect sawdust and protect fingers and knees from the so-called hidden part of the blade. The saw which comes closest to meeting these specifications is either the Powermatic Model 66, or any of several brands built prior to 1960. For economic reasons, manufacturers are now cutting corners, and the result is a poor approximation of what used to be. We have two Deltas in the shop, side by side. One was built back in the fifties, the other is three years old. The differences are unbelievable. The new one has a cheap aluminum miter fence, no locking device on the rear of the parallel fence, and an open undercarriage. It vibrates so badly that unless clamped firmly, any piece of wood setting idly on the table dances to the floor. The final

Miter fence with wooden extension. Note use of block and clamp for making multiple cuts of the same length.

irony is that the new saw costs approximately twice as much as the old one.

A minimum set of saw blades would include rip, crosscut, combination, and planer blades along with a dado set and a moulding cutter. If sustained heavy-duty cutting is anticipated, then a carbide-tipped combination blade is a good investment. The carbide which cuts a rough kerf will hold an edge four or five times longer than a steel blade. Blades should be kept sharp and, with the exception of the planer blade, should have an adequate set. The planer blade has a thin-wall disc and should not require set. If a blade gets gummed up, as it will do, particularly when pine and other pitchy woods are cut, either lacquer thinner or oven cleaner will clean it and save the operator considerable anguish.

There are other attachments for the table saw which are worth considering. The tenon-cutting jig is useful in cutting straight, parallel tongues; however, a skilled craftsman can achieve the same accuracy by his natural sense of plumb and trained dexterity. One or two finger springs can

be made to provide an even and safe pressure forcing the stock down and toward the fence. These are useful when cutting multiple pieces, particularly mouldings. Another aid easily built is the tapering jig. When cutting tapered table legs, for example, this tool is invaluable.

Today all saws come equipped with safety guards. Even though the new ones are made of clear plastic, the operator still has great difficulty seeing his work with the guard down. It quickly becomes a burden and can be downright dangerous. One can also be lulled into a false sense of security with the guard in place. This should be remembered: if wood can pass beneath the guard, so can the fingers. The best safety device is the good sense of the operator. I have made an informal study of saw accidents and have determined that most occur under two circumstances. First, somebody walks into the room as a man is passing a board through; he looks up to say good morning and loses a fingertip. Hence, *never take your eyes off the blade*. Second, the stock begins to rise or bind or the cut is near its end and the operator reaches behind the blade to pull it through. The blade kicks the stock forward and pulls the hand with it. Hence, *never reach behind a rotating blade.*

Radial Arm Saw: A much overrated tool, the radial arm saw is only helpful in crosscut work. Although it ostensibly adjusts to do everything from planing to ripping, these processes take time to set up and when made are quite difficult to execute. Another disadvantage, even with the most expensive models, is their inability to hold accurate settings. As the various bearings wear, the saw loses accuracy in indexing and must be adjusted with try square and miter gauge each time a new setup is made. However, as a cut-off saw or right-angle dado saw, the radial arm saw is unsurpassed because the operator can see his work from the top.

Band Saw: Band saws are classed by size based on the distance of the blade from the framework of the saw itself (throat). A 16-inch or 20-inch throat is adequate for most small operations where thickness requirements of six or seven inches are the maximum. Multispeed capacity is not necessary, since this feature applies more to cutting plastic and metal. Two sizes of blades, ¼ inch and ½ inch, should be on hand. The ¼-inch, although easily broken, allows much tighter turns, down to 1½-inch diameter. The ½-inch blade is much more durable and should be used most of the time. When a band saw blade breaks, have it rewelded. This might be repeated three or four times until the blade becomes dull; it should then be discarded.

Most band saws have a slot for a miter gauge which can be used to achieve moderate accuracy. A more useful accessory is a simple wooden extension with a sharp pin located tangent to the blade. This provides a pivot upon which perfectly round discs of any dimension may be cut.

Jigsaw: Unless one produces ornamental scroll-

Cutting short dados with the radial arm saw.

54

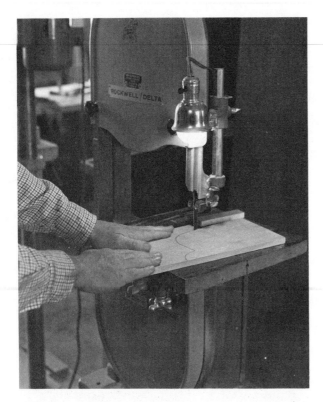

Above: small shop bandsaw.

Jigsaw cutting an inside hole.

work or jigsaw puzzles, this tool is strictly a shop luxury. We rarely use ours on Shaker designs, preferring the humble coping saw.

Jointer: In two passes over the jointer virtually any ripped edge can be flattened and straightened sufficiently for gluing. The jointer is also useful in flattening twisted or cupped boards which can then be passed either through a surface planer or, if relatively narrow, vertically through a table saw. It also provides an excellent means of squaring two edges of a board which can then be fenced on a table saw for ripping.

For most small operations the six-inch jointer is quite adequate, providing it has a long bed (at least 48 inches overall), a fence capable of lateral and tilted settings, and a full three-quarter horsepower motor which develops a cutterhead speed of 4000 r.p.m.

Spindle Shaper: In a small shop the work of a spindle shaper is performed by hand moulding planes, the portable router, or the moulding head on a table saw. However, these processes can be performed most efficiently on a spindle shaper. Running at 10,000 r.p.m., the three edged knives of this tool cut clean profiles of almost limitless contour and size. Since the direction of rotation can be changed, it can cut without tearing against the grain. The cost of this tool, however, is considerable. The hobbyist should not consider it essential; besides, working with an old moulding plane can be fun.

Lathe: The simplest and probably the oldest of all power tools is the wood-turning lathe. The Egyptians used lathes powered by a bowstring, which in turn was powered, no doubt, by an apprentice who pulled and pushed as the master guided the knife. Today's lathe is fundamentally the same, except that an electric motor spins the stock in one direction only at a predetermined speed. A good lathe, for general purposes, should have adjustable speeds and at least a six-inch clearance between the center of the headstock and the top of the bed. Also, in order to turn almost any rear chair leg there should be a potential 42 inches between headstock and tailstock. Unfortunately, no lathes built for home use allow a

Six-inch jointer.

swing of more than 36 inches. The only way to accommodate a longer swing is by bolting on another lathe bed or jury-rigging an extension to hold the tailstock.

A set of six or eight turning tools is necessary. Except for gouges these can be made from discarded files. My favorite lathe tool is a $5/16$-inch roundnose ground from a broken screwdriver which I cut and retempered.

Drill Press: The variable-speed drill press is a versatile tool which is used almost every day in our shop. It bores holes with absolute precision. In addition, the mortise adaptor converts the drill press into a hollow chisel mortiser which, to the delight of the uninitiated, cuts square holes. To be sure, the foot-operated, heavy-duty mortising machine is much preferred for heavy production work. However, unless used in straight production, the drill press mortise adaptor is more than sufficient.

Stationary Disc Sander: Having tried a six-inch stationary belt sander and, of course, the three-inch portable types, we have concluded that for smoothing end grain and convex edges the simple disc sander is the most efficient. Fitted with a 60 or 100 grit disc, this sander has saved countless hours and tempers in the tedious task of smoothing endgrain.

Stroke Sander: For smoothing large panels the stroke sander provides the best job—unless, of course, one can afford a multi-drum or industrial grade self-feeding drum sander. With a little practice one can learn to achieve absolute flatness using the stroke sander. Abrasive manufacturers make a wide range of belt sizes and, with time and ingenuity, one can make his own stroke sander using wooden drums. The one pictured uses a six-inch belt 168 inches long and has a table which passes back and forth under the belt.

Pneumatic Sander: Also called a balloon

56

speed industrial type surface planer is so well designed that when properly adjusted it turns out polished wood which scarcely needs sanding. A new tool is now being introduced to replace the planer altogether. A massive belt sander with long-lived abrasives, it can remove up to ¼ inch of stock in hardwood in one pass.

For the small shop, surface planers are made in graduated sizes from twelve inches to thirty inches. Although the small one is capable of surfacing almost any board which is commercially available, it is too narrow to receive a glued-up chest side or tabletop. The larger one is probably larger than necessary when weighing the number of times it is used versus its cost. Accordingly, we use an eighteen-inch surface planer through which we can pass any single board and most box and case components. In building a tabletop we glue up two halves, neither of which is more than

sander, this tool consists of two rubber cylinders with solid ends which can be inflated with air. By varying the air pressure, soft or sharp contours can be sanded. When fitted with a coarse belt, 40 or 60 grit, it can rough out complicated sculptured parts in short order. However, considerable practice is necessary in mastering this tool. Again, it is possible to buy the drums and fit them to an arbor and power source of your own invention.

Surface Planer: Planers come in various frame types; some are portable, most are stationary. Here again a good axiom is, the heavier the better. The old-fashioned planers with the enormous cast steel frames are magnificently sturdy but usually come with babbit bearings and square 2-knife heads. The babbit bearings are usually worn and difficult or impossible to replace, while the square heads are dangerous at best and usually leave a rough surface. On the other hand, the new high-

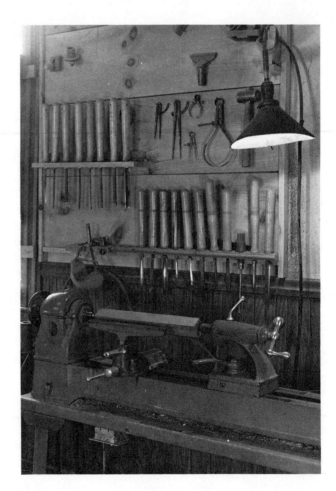

Thirty-six inch lathe with tools.

eighteen inches wide. After these are surfaced, they in turn are glued up to make a top up to thirty-six inches wide.

A planer, to operate effectively, should be properly vented and chip free, otherwise one is forever shoveling shavings. It is also a good idea to have an extra set of knives on hand so that no down time is experienced when the blades are being sharpened.

Bench Grinder: No shop should be without a high-speed (3450 r.p.m.) grinder for making and sharpening tools. One arbor should be equipped with a coarse stone used for rough shaping while the other should be equipped with a 54G, grade K aluminum oxide stone for high-speed sharpening. For other kinds of processes, such as buffing and polishing and steel brushing, a buffing lathe or simple arbor setup should be used.

This finishes my discourse on power tools. Obviously, there are many tools which I have left out of this listing and, no doubt, there are probably several here that can be done without very nicely. However, these are the tools that have found a place in our operation. With a few exceptions the stationary tools have been bought second-hand. Used portable tools are a little like automobiles—someone else's trouble. With the heavier tools, such as the planer, jointer, disc sander, and so on, there are very few moving parts, and these tools, when reconditioned, are as good or better than new ones. A well-worn heavy-duty old tool, well calibrated and with good bearings, is better than a new lightweight model which costs three or four times as much. Finally, if a new tool is purchased, stay away from the cheap, "nationally advertised" Christmas special at $18.99. A good tool should be an investment and, as it is written, a joy forever.

The Work Bench

Sad to say, there are many woodworking shops, specializing in everything from captain's chairs to lobster traps, in which there cannot be found a single workbench. Each step in the process of manufacture is so highly specialized that an old-fashioned bench simply isn't needed. In our shop each man has his own bench designed to fit his

Drill press.

own needs. One has a tool tray, another a pine top devoid of any permanent accoutrements. Yet another bench is of hardwood with double wood vise and elaborate steel dogs and stops. The height of working surfaces varies, too, according to need.

Two of us keep our hand tools in specially designed vertical boxes, while another uses the old-fashioned toolbox. My tools, because most of them are also used as general shop tools, are kept on open shelves and racks.

Shop Layout

Bench type, shop layout, and tool storage are highly individual matters. Given this premise, let us explore the "ideal" one-man workshop.

It should have a wood floor which is easy on the feet and can be nailed into and swept. There should be plenty of windows for light and air cir-

Stationary disc sander.

Stroke sander: the table rolls back and forth under the belt.

culation. Clear incandescent lights should flood the room on dark days, and in a northern climate there should be a wood-burning stove, well protected with asbestos insulation, for burning scraps and taking the chill off, as well as for controlling dampness. Work spaces should be arranged so that one's back is always to the window in order to avoid glare. If there is much power equipment, particularly sanders, an exhaust system should be installed to remove dust and shavings; otherwise, individual machines should be fitted with vacuum type canisters. The floor space in front of each machine should be wide open; and if the floor is slippery, a rubber mat should be in place to provide leg and foot stability during the operation of machines. Although most stationary tools, such as table saws, jointers, and drill presses, can be shifted to allow for the clear pass of a long piece of lumber, every effort should be made to place these tools so that the stock will clear, fore and aft, and to each side. The table heights should also be pretty much the same so that a board can pass from one on to another. Remember, the longest raw lumber is sixteen feet and a finished case will rarely extend beyond eight feet.

The finishing room should be away from the shop area, and no flammable material should be allowed in the shop proper. There should always be several fire extinguishers in plain view. In our shop we keep an ordinary garden hose connected and ready at all times. All drive belts and pulleys should be covered with guards and all electrical circuits should be double-grounded. There should be plenty of outlets, both 115 and 230 volts. When possible, fixed machinery should be wired for 230, since that will result in an over-all energy savings. All benches should be equipped with duplex power boxes, and the floor should be as free of extension cords as possible. There should be a master switch, under lock and key, to control all power equipment in the shop. When not in use, equipment should be inoperable. Walls and ceilings should have acoustical properties, possibly acoustical tile, at least on the ceiling. Although power equipment saves time, it does not do the same for eardrums.

In addition to a vise-equipped workbench, there should be an assembly table made of softwood into which one can nail jigs without suffering pangs of conscience. Needless to say, this should be as flat as possible. A good size would be 36 inches by 96 inches, although a much smaller size will work. For trimming the bottoms of chairs and table legs, and for other applications where an absolutely flat surface is required, the table saw table is usually adequate. There should be at least one pair of saw horses at the ready for assembling large case pieces. The tops of these can be covered with old carpeting to prevent scratching. The novice is inclined to work on the floor on hands and knees, but should resist this at all costs: use saw horses, benches, and tables.

There should be a set of racks for holding clamps according to length. Nearby should be the clamping table upon which panel gluing is performed. If space limitations don't permit a separate table, then the rack can be fitted to the saw horses. In any case, gluing should not be done on one's workbench, where a clean, glue-

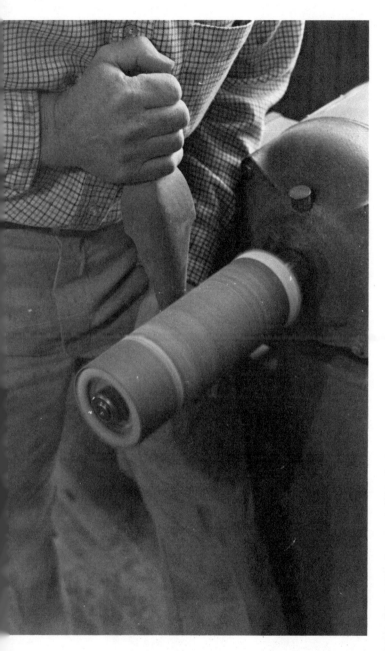

Pneumatic sander: air pressure adjusts to sand special contours.

Feeding the 18-inch surface planer.

free surface must always be maintained.

All scrapwood should be stored either vertically in small bins where it can be seen from at least three sides or horizontally in racks where it can also be seen. Without visibility, one soon forgets what is on hand and finds it easier to cut a new piece from the storage stock. It's a good idea to cull out scrap wood from time to time lest it take over like a strangling vine.

Floor layout depends on the amount of equipment and the space available. My smallest workshop, a back porch in Michigan, was approximately four feet by twelve feet and had a permanent laundry sink fixed on one wall. There was sufficient room only for a small table saw, yet in that space I built several grandfather clocks, toy boxes, and a two-piece pewter cupboard of generous proportion. While sawing it was necessary to pass the board through an open window, but it worked! Our shop is now fifty feet by seventy feet, on three floors, and we still don't have enough room.

In laying out a shop keep traffic flow in mind. Conceptually, one must go from rough board to planed board to rip saw to jointer to glue rack. Then from glue rack to plane to surface sander to workbench to assembly bench to finishing room. If the layout doesn't come clear, ask your wife to lay out the ideal kitchen. If she's a good cook, she should have no trouble. Then simply follow her methodology.

Unquestionably, the most frustrating outside influence on the cabinetmaker is the vacillation between high and low humidity brought on by the changing seasons. We have a humidistat in our wood storage area which shows an average humidity of 40 percent during the winter and 90 percent during the summer and spring. Kiln-dried and air-cured wood should be stored at a constant 50 percent. In order to achieve this we use a humidifier in the winter (mounted in the plenum of our hot-air furnace) and a dehumidifier in the spring. In spite of our efforts extremes occur.

Several years ago I bought a small sailboat and told a friend that it was a compromise until we could afford a bigger one. He smiled knowingly and said, "Every boat is a compromise." And so it is with a workshop. No matter how well equipped, to the lover of fine tools it is always a compromise.

Bench grinder.

This work table measures 38" x 96" and has a 2-inch pine top.

Bill Huston's bench, which he built as a student in Norway. This is a typical example of the European work bench.

Chapter 4

Building Processes

Options

The notion that you should not burn bridges behind you is a serviceable nostrum for many activities in life (except possibly strategic retreat in war). Applied to cabinetmaking it means, *leave your options open*; or, don't cut a board until you have to. When planning the steps in building a piece of furniture, particularly a complex piece, finding the proper sequence can make the difference between success and failure. In building a house one proceeds with the foundation, subfloor, walls, ceiling beams, roof, outside finish, and, finally, inside finish. The same is true with certain classes of furniture, only one doesn't start from the bottom and work up. In building case pieces, a four-sided carcass (two sides, top, bottom) is built first, then backs, fronts, legs, and trim are added. In building a table, the legs are built first, then the apron or stretchers, and finally the top is fitted to the base. In building a drawer, it is front first, then sides and back, and finally, almost as an afterthought, the bottom is added.

In each situation considerable effort is saved by following a sequence. However, at every step, succeeding steps must be taken into account and prepared for. Even though a case carcass consists of only six parts, these, particularly the sides, must be fitted with the various dado, rabbet, and dovetail cuts necessary for sliding in shelves and drawer dividers, and backs and fronts, and so on. If one waits until after the carcass is put together

to make these cuts, his task will be manifestly more difficult. Similarly, in building a stretcher-based table it is possible to fit the stretchers to the legs *after* the legs are permanently joined to the apron, but at considerable effort and usually in a compromised way with marginal results.

A fitting analogy here might be to the Cadillac dashboard light-replacement scandal! Whether apocryphal or not, the story goes that according to the labor manual put out by General Motors several years ago the standard charge for replacing a particular dashboard light bulb in a then new Cadillac was $40.00. Fifteen cents for the bulb and $39.85 for labor. Four hours work is required to change the bulb. Even automotive engineers don't always think ahead.

Always keep your options open. Never cut a piece of wood until you have to. Do not study one of the following plans and proceed to cut out all 172 parts and then expect them all to fit together. If you do rough out your parts, always leave them an inch or two longer and wider than necessary. You can always trim a little off but you cannot add to the length of a piece of wood. Panels can be glued up and made as wide as you please, but until some genius invents the lineal board stretcher, boards, once cut off, cannot be lengthened.

The most important consideration in laying out parts is wood color and grain characteristics. If the material is on hand, drawer fronts should be cut from the same board. Stiles and rails should have the same color and graining patterns. Remember, a simple wipe with a cloth dampened in paint thinner will show the finished color.

Gluing Up Panels

There are three or four variables that affect how individual boards are placed within a glued-up panel. Once ripped and joined and matched for color, and after sapwood and other gross imperfections are cut away, the clearest sides are placed face up on the clamps resting on the gluing rack. Small, tight knots and other minor imperfections can be left on an outside surface and can be repaired later. If only 100 percent clear wood is used, the proportion of waste would be simply too great. Besides, small knots and crotch grain add interest and character. To minimize future cupping, the ideal arrangement is to alternate grain patterns. If this unduly affects color and clarity of grain, it need not be performed.

White glue, Titebond, or liquid hide glue should be liberally applied to all inside joints. Bar clamps are placed eight inches to twelve inches apart, alternating top and bottom. If they are all placed on one side, under sufficient pressure the whole panel will buckle up out of the rack. To make sure the bottom of the panel is flat, bring all the pieces flush to the bar clamps by using a mallet or C-clamp before the final tightening of the bar clamps. Never glue up in temperatures below 60°F., and always leave your work in the clamps for at least a couple of hours. In humid conditions more time might be necessary. Although the

GLUING PANELS

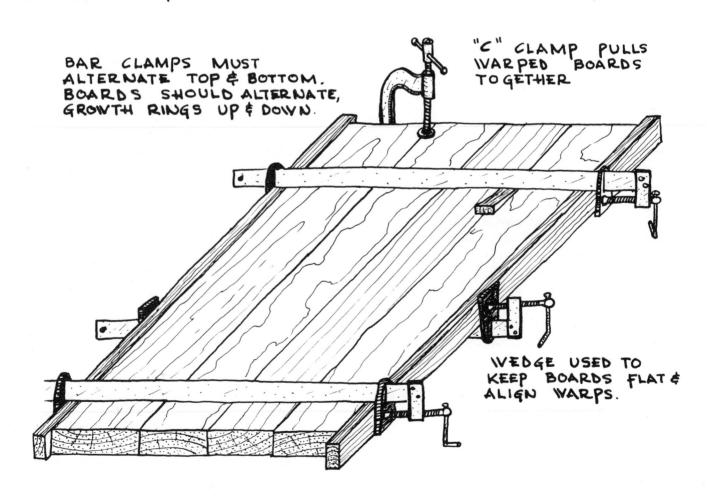

BAR CLAMPS MUST ALTERNATE TOP & BOTTOM. BOARDS SHOULD ALTERNATE, GROWTH RINGS UP & DOWN.

"C" CLAMP PULLS WARPED BOARDS TOGETHER

WEDGE USED TO KEEP BOARDS FLAT & ALIGN WARPS.

BUTT JOINTS: CORNER

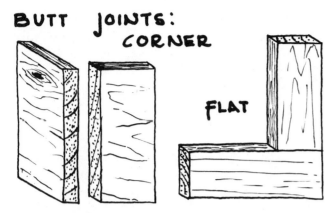

FLAT

RABBET JOINTS: SINGLE

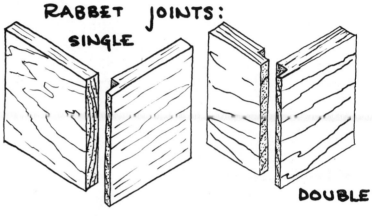

DOUBLE

DADO JOINTS:

PLAIN

BLIND OR STOPPED

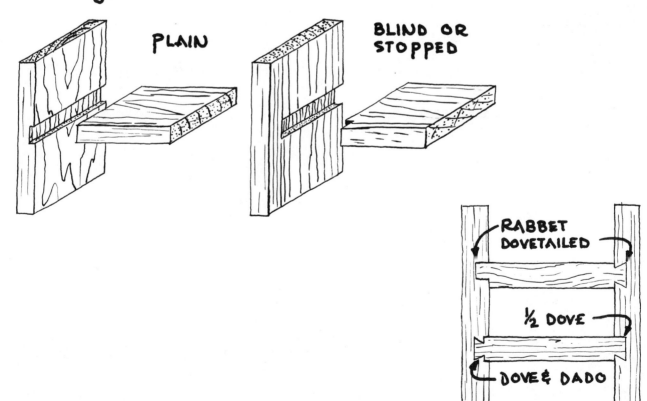

RABBET DOVETAILED

½ DOVE

DOVE & DADO

LAP JOINTS:

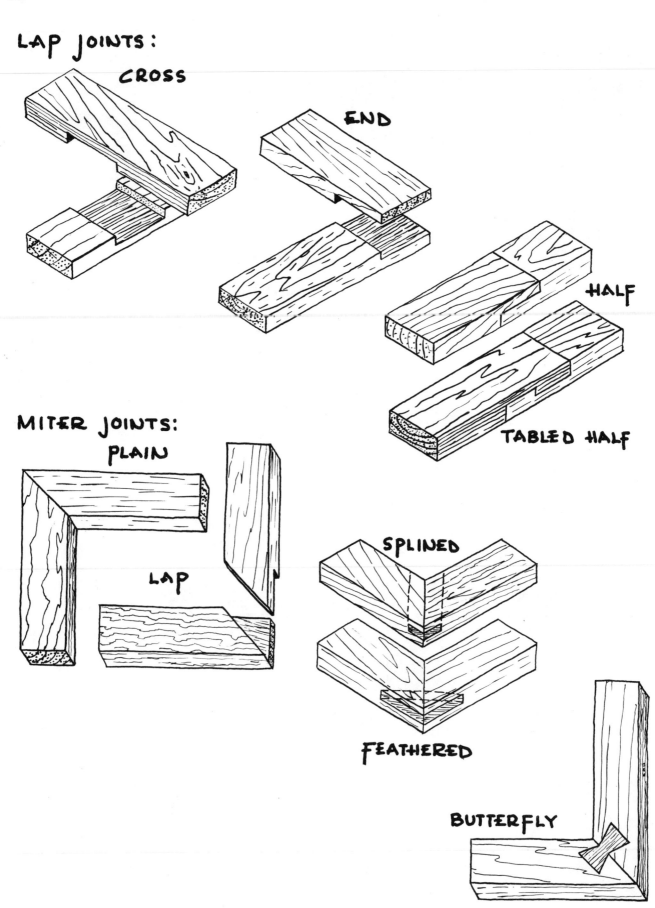

CROSS

END

HALF

TABLED HALF

MITER JOINTS:

PLAIN

LAP

SPLINED

FEATHERED

BUTTERFLY

MORTISE & TENON JOINTS:

PLAIN   STUB
         (THROUGH)

PEGS

BARE-FACED   THROUGH

KEYED   THROUGH & WEDGED

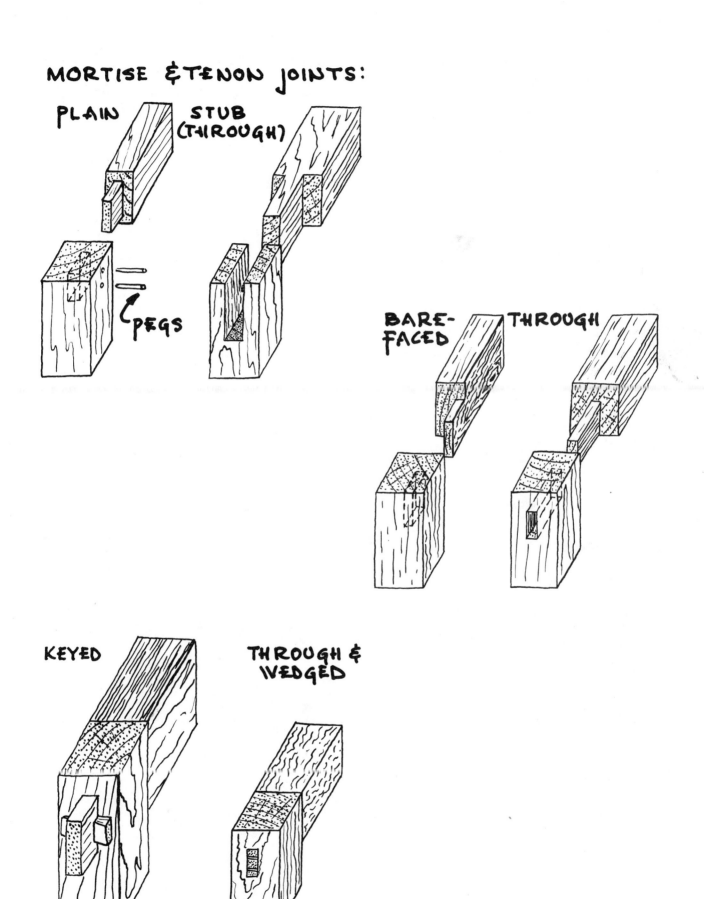

FOX WEDGED

BOX OR FINGER JOINT:

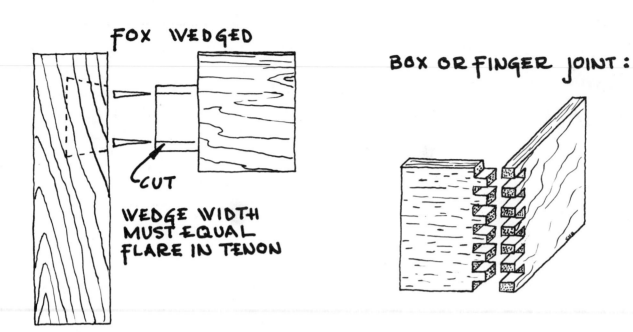

CUT

WEDGE WIDTH
MUST EQUAL
FLARE IN TENON

DOVETAIL JOINTS:

SIMPLE OR
THROUGH

1 INCH

10°

6 INCHES

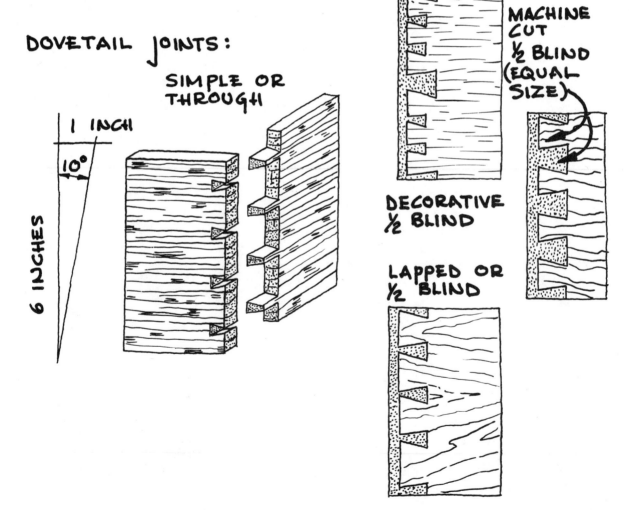

MACHINE
CUT
½ BLIND
(EQUAL
SIZE)

DECORATIVE
½ BLIND

LAPPED OR
½ BLIND

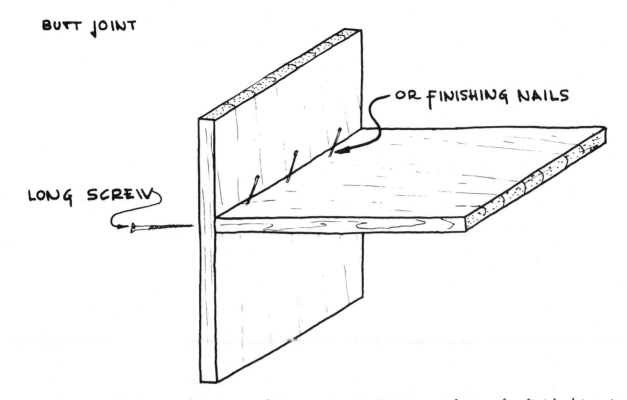

BUTT JOINT

OR FINISHING NAILS

LONG SCREW

clamp pressure will bring almost anything together, the tighter the joint at the outset, before pressure is applied, the better. If properly done this panel may break under force, but not at the glue joints. When dry, the excess glue should be scraped off and the panel smoothed with jack plane or surface planer and sanded, both sides, to 120 grit (120 is satisfactory for finished interior and secondary surfaces). The panel is now ready for dressing to exact dimensions and other joint preparation and should be clamped in a flat position until ready for assembly. If a number of panels are stacked, stickers should be placed between them to maintain flatness.

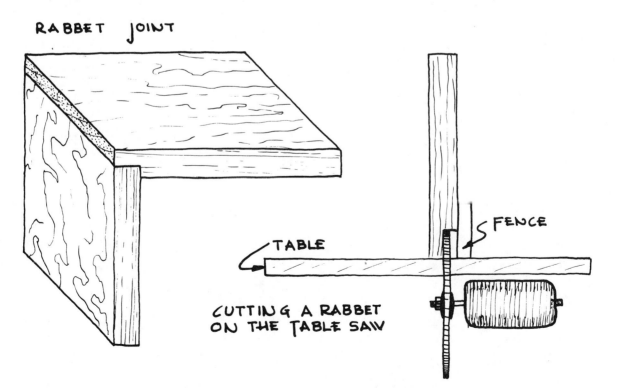

RABBET JOINT

FENCE

TABLE

CUTTING A RABBET
ON THE TABLE SAW

Joint Construction

Marking and Scribing: For general marking a medium-fine pencil is satisfactory, though some persons recommend the flat carpenter's pencil. When extreme accuracy is required, a scribing knife or awl should be used. It is also wise to mark on the work which side the saw or chisel is to cut. Even professionals forget and cut out the wrong material on a set of dovetails or put a dado on the wrong side of a scribe line. When permanently numbering joints that are designed to come apart, such as on bedposts or knockdown tables, a set of Roman numerals cut carefully with a ⅜-inch chisel makes a permanent mark. Drawers of the same dimensions should also be so numbered, possibly on their undersides.

Butt Joint: The least effective, though certainly the quickest, the butt joint gains its strength by nails or screws with a minimum of glued surface. The greater the surface area of contact the stronger will be the joint, especially if glue is used.

The butt joint is occasionally used in secondary joints and often in applying trim which is nonstructural.

Rabbet Joint: An excellent joint for fitting cases together and for insetting backs is the rabbet joint. When properly glued and clamped, the seams can be made tight; but clamping is awkward since pressure has to be applied in two directions. This joint is best made on the table saw. Using the parallel fence, first make one cut, then the other. Notice that the strip to be cut out is between blade and fence, making it impossible to overcut the joint.

Tongue and Groove: Used widely in house construction (matched floors, wall and roof sheathing, and so on), the tongue and groove is used in furniture principally to fit together the back of a case. If extremely accurate machining is available, this joint can be used in a glued-up panel. The tongue is cut as though it were two rabbets, while the groove is cut by multiple passes

CUTTING TONGUE & GROOVE JOINT ON THE TABLE SAW

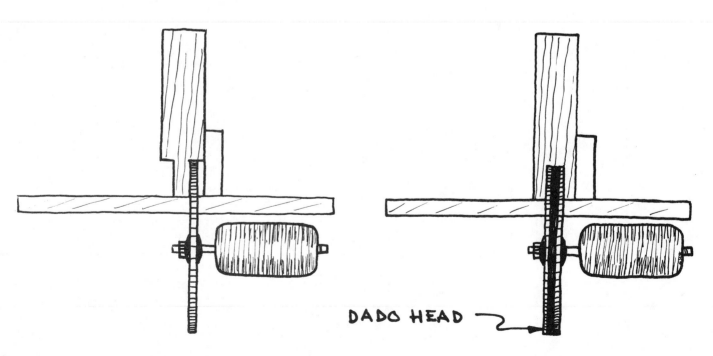

DADO HEAD

SPLINE JOINT DETAIL

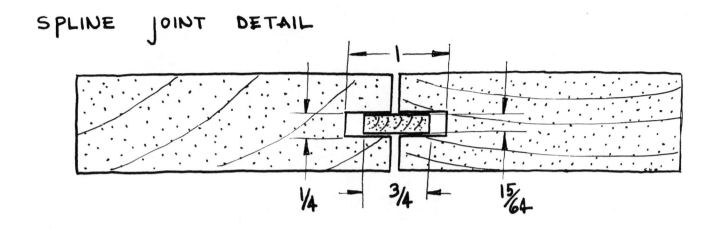

over the saw blade or by using a dado head. To cut these joints by hand, you would use a rabbet plane and moulding plane or backsaw.

Spline: Preferred over the tongue and groove, since board width is not diminished when used, the spline joint is an excellent means of joining two members. With a floating spline in place, the wood is allowed to swell and shrink without having daylight pass through. The spline itself, made of scrapwood, should be slightly thinner than dado cuts and should be finished (stained, painted, or whatever) before being slipped into the slot.

Dovetail: The dovetail joint achieves its beauty by piercing a flat surface with darker endgrain. Considerable strength is achieved, and the joint can only be pulled apart in one direction. When glued, this joint is almost impossible to break. Full dovetails are used on corners, whereas some drawer fronts, rails, and stiles usually take half-blind dovetails.

Both pieces are cut to full length, or possibly a

DOVETAILS

FULL OR THROUGH

HALF BLIND OR LAPPED

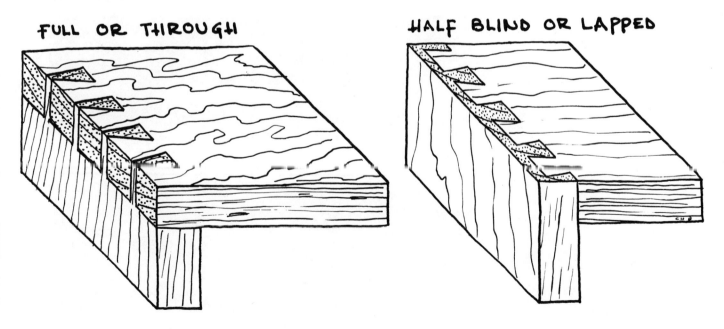

This series of photos shows
how dovetails are marked
out.

Steps in laying out dovetails
using a simple system for
achieving equal intervals. The
scale is marked on the stock.

Lines are drawn from marks to
edge in parallel.

The thickness of the other
board is scribed.

sixteenth-inch longer than necessary, and fully squared. With the scribing gauge both sides of each piece are marked to indicate the depth of the impending cuts. Using a bevel square or a marking template the female slots are marked out on the edge of the top. These should be evenly spaced and located so as to conceal rabbet or dados. A simple, equal-interval spacing method is to use a stick graduated at equal intervals from one to four inches. Lay this on a diagonal across the work so that the marks are equal in number to the desired number of dovetails. Transfer the marks to the work and, using either a try square or framing square, draw parallel lines from these marks to the edge. No matter what width you are dealing with, the marks will have equal intervals. A try square is then used to drop a straight line to meet the scribe line. Using a backsaw, or a bandsaw if one is available, cuts are made on the *inside* of these marks to the scribe line. Finally, using an appropriate chisel, waste is removed.

Having completed the females, the matching male section is marked out by using the finished female as a template. A knife or sharp hard pencil is used, and again the sections to be cut out are marked with an X. Vertical lines are again dropped to the scribe line and the process of sawing and chiseling is repeated. Cut on the outside of knife marks in order to achieve a tight fit. It is always possible to trim away if it's too tight, but hard to add wood once it is cut. Occasionally, a miscut can be repaired by forcing a sliver taken from the same board into the gap, but this should only be done on a joint not readily seen.

Doweled Joint: In the modern factory almost all joints are made with specially fluted dowels. The result is a slightly improved butt joint, which in time will come apart. To conceal this economy, some manufacturers add a false peg to make it look as though the joint is really a pinned mortise and tenon. Sadly, this usually isn't discovered until after the dowel has shrunk—as it most certainly will in time—and the piece has fallen apart. I can only recommend the use of the dowel joint to give added strength to panel glue joints, particularly for table leaves.

Mortise and Tenon: Doors, windows, drawer dividers, table bases, breadboarded tabletops, bed

Above: bevel square is used to mark out female dovetails.

Below: the dovetail edges are squared.

This series shows the complete dovetails.

Above: female dovetails are cut, keeping saw inside sharp scribe marks.

Above: female dovetails are cleaned out with bevel chisel.

Below: using females as a template, marks are scribed onto the other section of the joint.

joints, and a host of other components are built with the mortise and tenon (think: mortise = mouth, tenon = tongue). When the tongue passes completely through the mortise stock, it is called a revealed tenon, which is usually further tightened by one or more wedges for additional strength. (Note: Never drive a wedge running parallel to the grain in the mortise stock or splitting will result.) Tenons can be square, rectangular, round, or any other shape—they are still tenons. Commonly, tenons are fitted, glued, and pinned as an extra precaution. Most eighteenth- and early nineteenth-century joiners did not glue these joints, and even today most door stiles and rails are not glued.

After deciding on how much depth the joint should have, or indeed, whether it should be revealed, the shoulders of the tenon are laid out with a try square and cut either with backsaw or on the table saw. A clean, square cut is necessary if the joint is to be tight. The tongue itself should be fairly smooth and of equal width and thickness along its length.

The tongue can then be positioned on the mortise stock and marked. This, in turn, is bored by auger and cleaned out and squared with a chisel. The tenon should fit snugly into its socket. If a

The male dovetails are squared.

X's are cut out, keeping inside of scribe mark.

Above: the pieces are joined. Bar clamps often help get a tight glue joint.

Below: paint thinner is wiped onto the wood to see if any glue residue remains after the joint has been sanded. Note that the scribe mark is left on as an added design feature.

drill press and hollow mortise chisel are used, all tenons are cut to standard thicknesses (¼ inch, ⅜ inch, and ½ inch).

When the mortise is quite long, more than six inches, as in the case of a breadboard or the deep apron of the standing desk, it can be cut on a table saw, with a dado head, and the ends cleaned out by chisel.

Building Case Pieces

A case is a six-sided box. Whether it is a tall clock, a cupboard, or a chest of drawers, it is, in its fundamental form, a box. Sides and top should be laid out so that the grain direction is consistent, allowing the inevitable shrinking and swelling to take place without breaking joints or splitting panels.

Before assembling the case, sides should be dadoed for shelves and dividers. Also, the interior rear inside edges should be rabbeted in preparation for inserting the back boards. If drawer frames are to be used, at least the lower frame should be fitted with a dust panel.

The top, bottom, and, in most cases, the shelves or dividers should be assembled at one time.

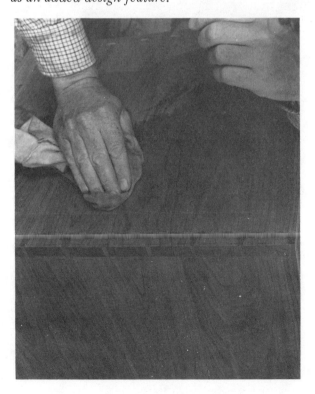

Placed on its front, on a pair of saw horses or other flat surface, the case should be squared by diagonal measurements from corner to corner and the back attached with nails or screws. It should then be turned over and front work can be done knowing that the carcass is square. If squareness is lost at any point during this process, every step beyond this, including the making of drawers, front frames, and hanging doors, will be made more difficult, since nothing will ever be square.

Building Tables

Most modern table and desk heights are 29 inches to 30 inches from floor to surface. There should be a minimum of 26 inches between floor and apron to accommodate legs and knees, and a generous place setting is 24 inches wide and 16 inches deep. These are universal dimensions and apply to all manner of designs. In addition, chair size and seating capacity are important. With a properly designed table one should never have to straddle a leg.

The construction sequence for the base begins with the legs, then apron, and finally stretchers. After all mortise and tenon joints are cut, the entire base is assembled at once. Here again the same rules for holding square apply. Prior to assembling the base, the method for applying it to the top must be determined and holes should be bored or mounting cleats should be fixed to the upper interior aprons. Since a tabletop will swell and shrink, it should never be fixed too firmly lest it split.

Tabletops are either fixed or expandable. In their fixed form they can be round, ovoid, square, or rectangular; in their expandable form they can have drop leaves or insert leaves or, I suppose, both. Having built a hundred dining tables, I would like to share certain generalizations that I have developed.

A round top with a diameter of greater than 52 inches is unworkable even if everyone present has

With the use of a dowelling jig, dowels can be driven in the exact center of an edge to be glued. The jig also helps in lineal alignment.

Cutting a tenon with backsaw.

THROUGH MORTISE & TENON, WEDGED

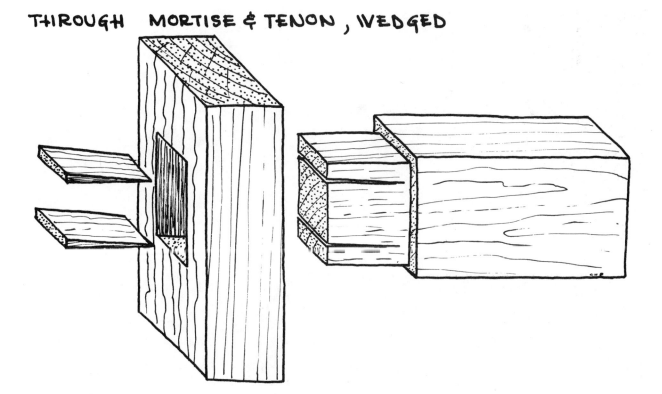

Above: drilling out a mortise.

Below: cleaning the mortise after boring.

a "boarding-house reach." When seated, even a tall man encounters difficulty in reaching beyond 38 inches, therefore 52 inches seems to be the logical limit. Our round dining table at home is 60 inches across, and although it works well for crowds, it isn't peaceful to eat at, since something is forever being passed.

Oval tables have great looking tops when long and narrow. However, if four legs are used, they are always awkwardly placed in this lean model. To broaden the stance of the base, the top must be made wider relative to its length, and one soon passes the aesthetic mean which defines an oval. Furthermore, if the oval table is designed to receive an inserted leaf, the leaf must be rectangular; and when the leaf is in place, the oval loses its unbroken curve. A well-executed oval table is a wonderful thing, but it is very easy to ruin a fine design with bad proportions.

Square tabletops are great on night stands and tables built for four people (36 inches by 36 inches minimum size). One built for eight or twelve

Fitting tenon to mortise.

MATCHING GRAIN DIRECTION

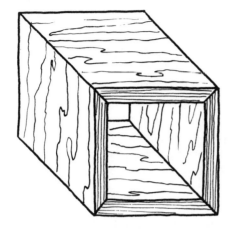 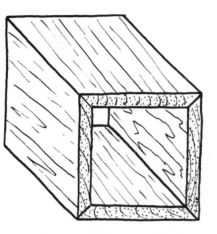

GRAIN RUNNING AROUND CASE CAUSES SHRINKAGE & EXPANSION FRONT TO BACK.

GRAIN RUNNING FRONT TO BACK CAUSES FACE TO SHRINK & EXPAND. PROBLEMS WITH DOOR & DRAWER FIT.

would have to come equipped with a small crane for reaching the center. Rectangular tops, on the other hand, offer limitless possibilities and always seem to work, providing the narrow dimension does not exceed 44 inches to 48 inches. Length, of course, is limited only by the size of the room. The Shakers made a group of communal dining tables twenty feet long and 34 inches wide for a dining hall in New Lebanon, New Hampshire.

Drop leaves are generally the most satisfactory, in that storage is no problem: they're always at hand and can be added or taken away with absolute ease. Numerous period antiques have drop leaves which extend almost to the floor. From an aesthetic point of view these are atrocious; they look a little like the maxi-dress that covers everything of interest above the ankle. The intermediate leaf, 16 inches or 18 inches wide, looks better, but has the drawback of falling below the level of a chair seat. Therefore, when not in the up position, the table does not permit any chairs to be placed under it, save possibly at the ends. The only truly workable leaf, then, is a 9-inch or 10-inch leaf which when up or down will receive a chair under it. Hence, the advent of the harvest table—a workable form.

Tables with insert leaves can be made to banquet hall proportions. By installing expandable sliders, as many as five 20-inch leaves can be added to a six-foot table, converting it to a fourteen-foot behemoth. The disadvantages of this form are (1) storing the leaves when not in use, (2) preventing the leaves from warping or twisting over the years with no longitudinal support, (3) installing and removing the multiple leaves, which can require not only patience but also a degree in mechanical engineering.

Drawer Construction

A properly fitted flush drawer should fit a carcass forwards, backwards, or upside down with equal clearance on all four sides. However, without a perfectly square opening to begin with it is doubtful that this can be achieved. Two kinds of drawers are found in our designs, one having a flush front, the other having a lipped front. While requiring a little more work in cutting the rabbets and edge moulding, the lipped drawer is easier to install since its quarter-inch overhang covers the opening and conceals any minor gaps that might otherwise appear. The flush drawer is easier to build but takes longer to fit to the case since absolute accuracy must be achieved. From an aesthetic point of view, the lipped drawer adds visual activity to a front, whereas the other achieves a surface flatness broken only by the pulls.

The front is first fitted to the case opening, then sides and back are cut to exact size. Planing and sanding usually reduces these by ⅛ inch in width, and this is a correct tolerance to guarantee ease of operation. If the drawer is particularly large, this tolerance should be increased to ³/₁₆ inches in order to accommodate seasonal expansion and contraction. Next, a dado is cut on the lower insides of the sides and front. Since most bottoms are ⅝ inches thick, the top of this dado should be about ¾ inch up the side to allow clearance be-

tween the drawer bottom and the chest rail. The dovetails are cut and fit, and lastly the bottom is sized and feathered either on the table saw or with a block plane and slid into place. The direction of grain on a drawer bottom should conform to the direction of the grain in the carcass. By making the drawer back narrower than the sides, the bottom can be slipped in from the rear after the drawer is assembled, and this is a considerable advantage. Once the drawer has been adjusted to operate smoothly, several finish nails can be driven through the bottom and into the back to hold the panel in place and keep the drawer square.

In a large chest the graduation of drawer sizes can help to give the piece a quality of stability while also providing for greater storage possibilities (deep drawers for sweaters and shallow

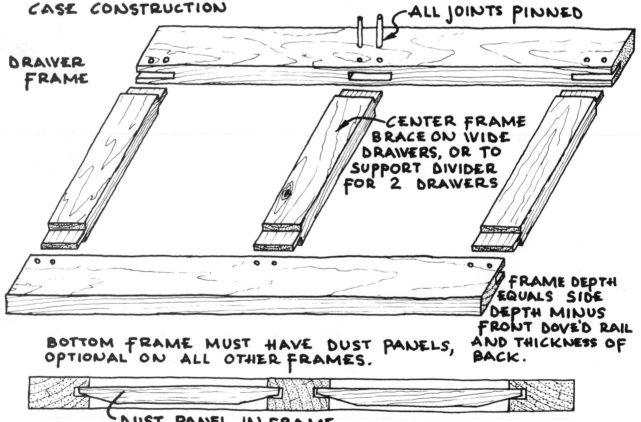

CASE CONSTRUCTION

ALL JOINTS PINNED

DRAWER FRAME

CENTER FRAME BRACE ON WIDE DRAWERS, OR TO SUPPORT DIVIDER FOR 2 DRAWERS

FRAME DEPTH EQUALS SIDE DEPTH MINUS FRONT DOVE'D RAIL AND THICKNESS OF BACK.

BOTTOM FRAME MUST HAVE DUST PANELS, OPTIONAL ON ALL OTHER FRAMES.

DUST PANEL IN FRAME

ones for handkerchiefs). Using a long wooden straight edge or a clean bench top, lay out the front, taking into account stile thickness and $^1/_{16}$ inch clearances. Determine the desired depth of the bottom drawer, say nine inches, or the depth of the top drawer, say 3½ inches, then through trial and error lay out the rest of the drawers in as close to one-inch graduations as possible.

Making and Hanging Doors

Door stiles and rails are cut first. For a better appearance the lower rail is usually wider, by ½ inch to 1 inch, than the top rail, while the top rail and both stiles are of equal width. Next, all four members receive a ¼-inch dado cut about ⅜ inch deep and centered in the stile and rail edge. Using

this trench as a guide, mortise and tenon joints are made. If a moulding is to appear on the door stiles and rails, it should be cut before the mortise and tenon joints. Once the frame is assembled, but before it is glued and pegged, the center panel is made to slide into the waiting dado slots. For a cupboard door of average size, the panel edge should penetrate all stiles and rails by about ¼ inch; on a larger door (more than 18 inches wide), the penetration should be closer to ⅜ inch in all directions.

One of the most frustrating steps in building a case can be hanging doors; such great labor is expended for apparently miniscule results. To avoid frustration, begin by fitting the door snugly on all four sides, it can later be planed down to the "nickel fit" (a properly hung door should have gaps on four sides just wide enough for one to

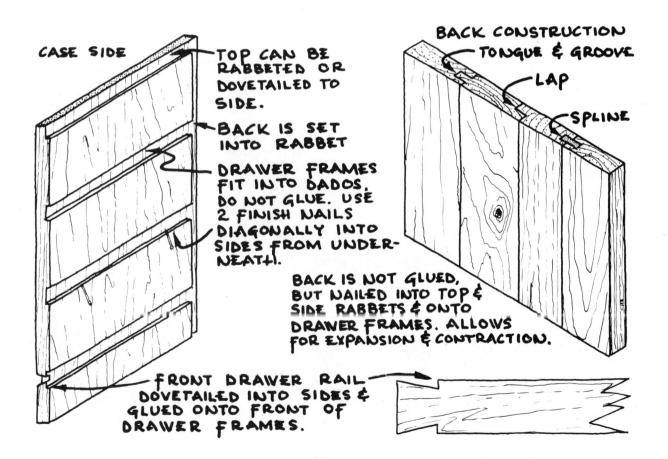

CASE SIDE

TOP CAN BE RABBETED OR DOVETAILED TO SIDE.

BACK IS SET INTO RABBET

DRAWER FRAMES FIT INTO DADOS. DO NOT GLUE. USE 2 FINISH NAILS DIAGONALLY INTO SIDES FROM UNDER-NEATH.

BACK CONSTRUCTION
TONGUE & GROOVE
LAP
SPLINE

BACK IS NOT GLUED, BUT NAILED INTO TOP & SIDE RABBETS & ONTO DRAWER FRAMES. ALLOWS FOR EXPANSION & CONTRACTION.

FRONT DRAWER RAIL DOVETAILED INTO SIDES & GLUED ONTO FRONT OF DRAWER FRAMES.

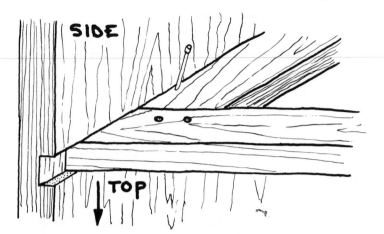

NAIL DRAWER FRAMES INTO PLACE.
USE 2 FINISH NAILS DIAGONALLY INTO
SIDE FROM BELOW. ATTACH TOP.

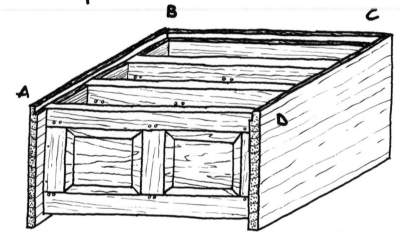

PLACE CASE FACE DOWN. ADJUST
CASE SO DIAGONAL MEASUREMENTS
A-C & B-D ARE EQUAL.

NAIL BACK INTO PLACE. COUNTER-
SINK ALL NAILS.

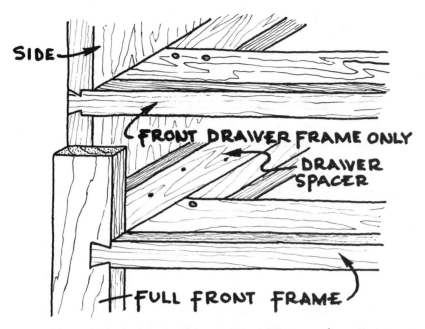

SIDE

FRONT DRAWER FRAME ONLY

DRAWER SPACER

FULL FRONT FRAME

APPLY ANY FRONT FRAMING & FRONT DRAWER FRAME RAILS. DOVETAIL INTO SIDES. APPLY ANY DRAWER SPACERS, DIVIDERS AND/OR DOOR STOPS.

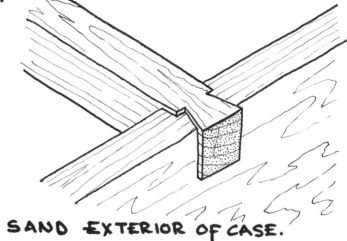

SAND EXTERIOR OF CASE.

GLUE.

NAIL

APPLY ANY MOULDING. ON SIDES GLUE ONLY FIRST FEW INCHES, NAIL THE REST. MAKE & FIT DOORS & DRAWERS. APPLY FINISH.

pass a nickel between door and case). A hinge leaf is then scribed onto the edge of the door three to five inches from top and bottom. Using a chisel and/or backsaw the hinge is inlet into the door stile. Once flush, the leaf is attached with only one screw (remember options: the hinge may have to be shifted slightly and a new hole drilled). When both hinges are in place, hold the door to the case and carefully mark where the hinge is to fit the case. Again, the hinge leaf is used in scribing the case stile. Rather than flush mounting, this leaf should be somewhat undercut in an effort to avoid later hinge binding.

After both hinges are in place and the door has been trimmed, the rest of the screws can be driven home. In trimming, it's a good idea to be mindful of the season. In the spring and summer we make tight fitting doors, in fall and winter, they are looser by as much as one-eighth inch, particularly if they are solid rather than panel doors.

Mouldings

There are countless ways to make mouldings, most of which were discussed in Chapter 3. Yet another method is to trace the intended moulding profile on the end grain of the rough stock. Then, by making multiple passes with a rip blade on the table saw, adjusting both fence and saw height each time, a complicated moulding can be roughed out. With scrapers, moulding planes, and sandpaper on curved blocks the moulding can be dressed and smoothed.

A simple way to make a cove is to clamp a board diagonally across the saw table just in front of the dado blade. By making repeated passes each time raising the blade slightly, a perfect ovoid flute can be cut which, when split in half, makes an excellent cove moulding.

In fitting mouldings to cases it is best not to cut all pieces at once and expect them to produce tight miter fits. By cutting and attaching one piece at a time, options are kept open, and the cuts are made only at the last moment.

Finishing Techniques

The key to success in applying a hand-rubbed finish is surface preparation. Most modern manufacturers process inadequately sanded wood by spraying a heavily pigmented, quick-drying synthetic finish over it. This hides surface imperfections and produces a finish smooth to the touch and water resistant. In time, of course, the finish will chip and crack with use, particularly if it is applied to a softwood such as pine, and the result is an ugly white scar which can be properly repaired only through complete refinishing. In producing a hand-rubbed finish more time and effort goes into sanding and surface preparation. Before a piece goes to the finishing room it should be machine-sanded to 120 grit and all marks made by earlier sanding grades should be completely removed on all exterior surfaces. Then with a slightly padded hand-sanding block all surfaces are further polished to 220 grit and edges and sharp corners are gently softened. Minor surface abrasions are filled with either tinted wood putty or, better yet, tinted stick shellac, which is melted into the cavity. Dents can be swollen back to the original surface level by placing a bead of hot water on the spot, or better, steam. As a last step, important surfaces can be lightly wiped with a water-soaked rag. This will raise minute surface wood fibers. When dry, the surface is finished with 220 and the entire piece is dusted and vacuumed and is finally ready for finish.

Oil Finish: The most natural looking finish, and the one most complimentary to wood, is the oiled finish. By heating the oil it becomes less viscous and penetrates deeper. (Turpentine and vinegar mixed with the oil will do the same thing, but this technique is less desirable since it dilutes the oil, making more applications necessary, and it is odorous.) Place an open container of boiled linseed oil on a hot plate and heat it to the point where it just begins to smoke. Remove it from the heat and apply it liberally to the prepared surface. Do not use a brush, since the bristles will curl. Rather, use a swab made of discarded cloth. After half an hour wipe all surfaces *completely dry*. It is essential that all excess oil be wiped off, since failure to do so will result in a permanently sticky condition: linseed oil never really hardens. If gumming does occur, a brisk rubbing of fine steel wool soaked in lacquer thinner will help. In a day or two, depending on drying conditions, sand with 220 grit or finer, and repeat. For most woods, four to six applications of oil are sufficient to give

METHODS OF ATTACHING TABLE BASE TO TOP

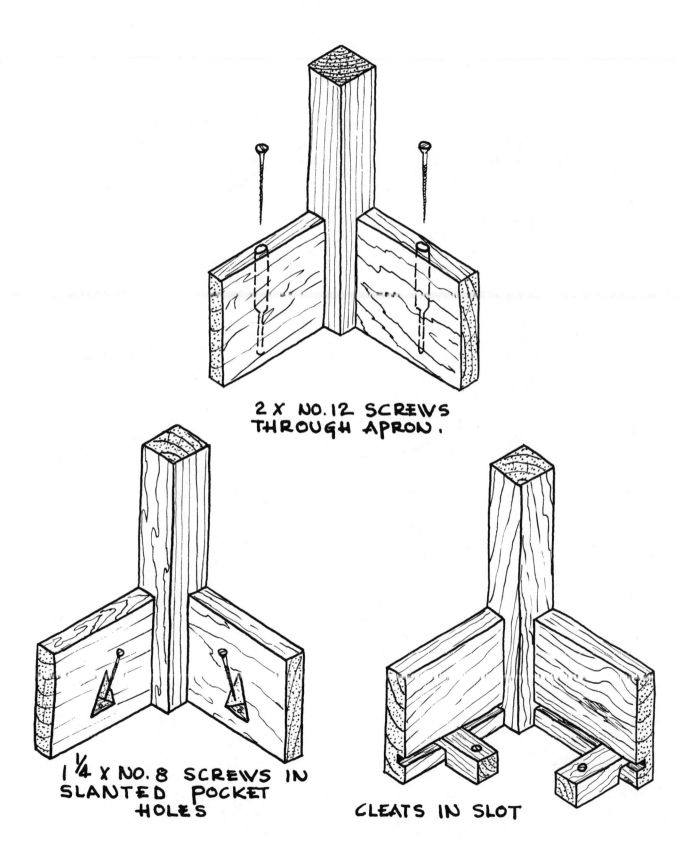

2 X NO.12 SCREWS
THROUGH APRON.

1¼ X NO. 8 SCREWS IN
SLANTED POCKET
HOLES

CLEATS IN SLOT

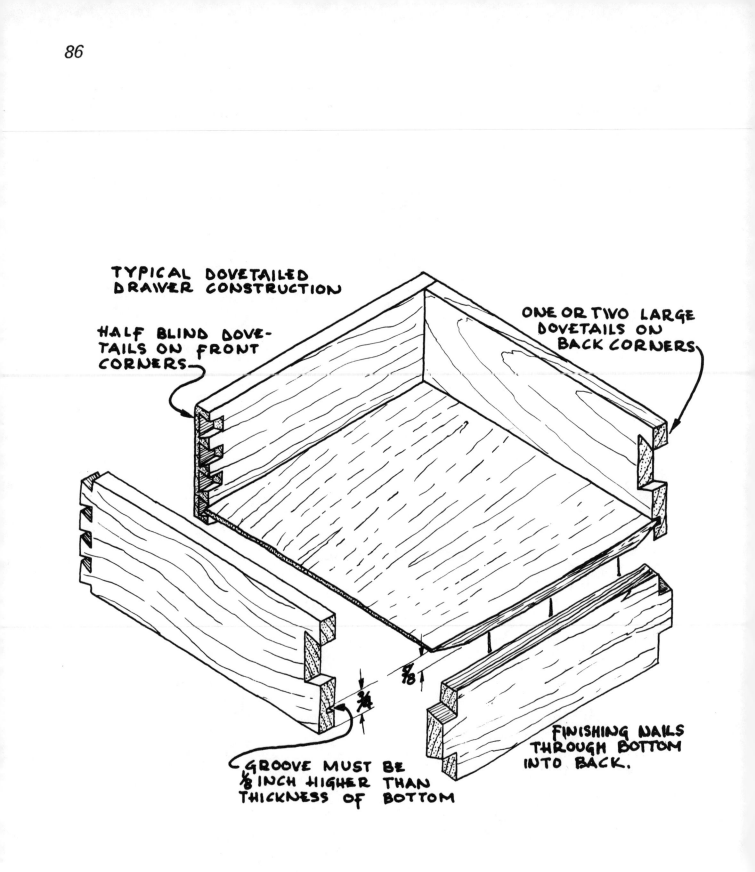

TYPICAL DOVETAILED
DRAWER CONSTRUCTION

HALF BLIND DOVE-
TAILS ON FRONT
CORNERS

ONE OR TWO LARGE
DOVETAILS ON
BACK CORNERS.

GROOVE MUST BE
⅛ INCH HIGHER THAN
THICKNESS OF BOTTOM

FINISHING NAILS
THROUGH BOTTOM
INTO BACK.

FLUSH DRAWER

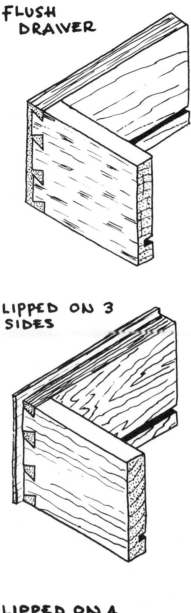

LIPPED ON 3 SIDES

LIPPED ON 4 SIDES

A set of lipped drawers, graduated and dovetailed by hand.

a build-up that will shine to a soft luster. After the last coat of oil has dried, apply a good quality wax (carnuba is best) using a 0000 steel wool pad as an applicator, let it dry half an hour and buff. Repeat this once or twice more for a satin-smooth, hand-rubbed oil finish capable of shedding water. This oiled finish is maintained by semiannual paste waxings. Even with periodic waxings the finish in time will pale and lose its vibrancy. When this occurs, perhaps every two years, a coat of hot linseed oil will break right through the wax and replenish the wood. Again, this oil should be wiped up thoroughly before rewaxing.

Although an oil finish brings out the best natural wood graining and accelerates the oxidation that causes the beautiful patina that comes with time, it is not a good finish to apply over heavily stained wood since, under these circum-

DOORS

TYPICAL RAISED
PANEL DOOR
CONSTRUCTION

RAIL

STILE

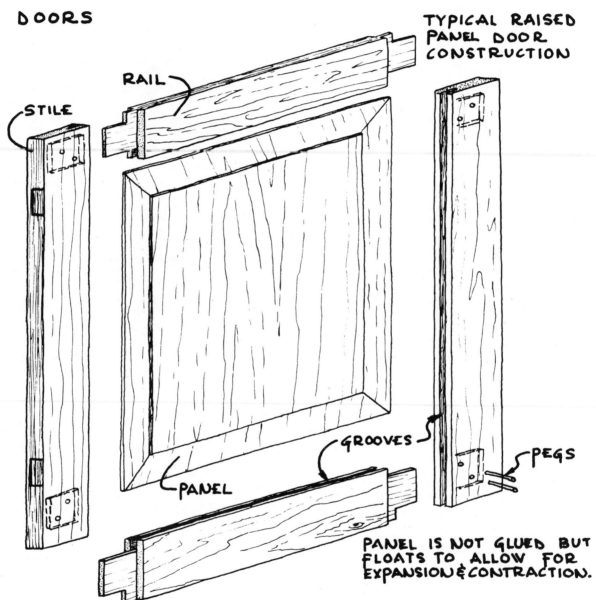

GROOVES

PEGS

PANEL

PANEL IS NOT GLUED BUT
FLOATS TO ALLOW FOR
EXPANSION & CONTRACTION.

PANEL TYPES:

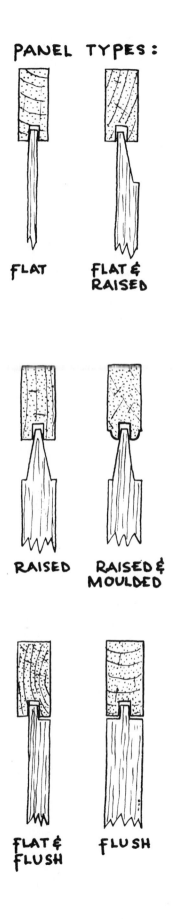

FLAT   FLAT &
           RAISED

RAISED   RAISED &
           MOULDED

FLAT &   FLUSH
FLUSH

stances, the finish will tend to become milky. For covering stained wood and for sealing out water a better finish is varnish.

Varnish: Natural and synthetic varnishes (polyurethane) are used when a highly shined and sealed surface is desired. After preparing the surface (as already described), the work is wiped completely with a tack cloth (treated cheesecloth) or a rag lightly dampened in paint thinner to remove all lint. The varnish, whether gloss or satin finish, should be stirred and passed through a fine paint sieve into a small can. Never brush varnish directly from the can it comes in lest you contaminate it with lint particles. And never use a varnish stain; they always look fake. If coloring must be done, a wiping stain should be applied to the raw wood. When the stain is fully dry, the varnishing process can begin. If you rush it, the stain will pull and mix with the varnish, particularly if the varnish is synthetic.

Using a natural bristle brush, apply an even coat. When dry, sand it vigorously with 220 production paper. After the second or third coat sand with 400 grit wet and dry paper, using either linseed oil or water as a lubricant. When completely smooth to the touch and free of all lint particles, the finish is ready to be rubbed out. Using 0000 steel wool, buff in the direction of the grain until an even luster appears. Now the piece can be waxed as already described. One caution is in order. Whenever buffing, either with steel wool or wet and dry paper, stay away from all edges lest you break through the membrane that has been building.

French Polish: A French polish is performed with shellac and linseed oil and applied to the prepared wood in a single pass. A cheesecloth pad is first soaked in boiled linseed oil, then lightly dipped into an open pan of orange or clear shellac. It is then applied to the wood by briskly rubbing back and forth. The oil works to lubricate the pad and a thin even coat of shellac is thus applied. With sufficient rubbing the shellac will dry almost immediately. The key is to get an even sheen, and this is very difficult to do on large flat surfaces. A French polish imbues the wood with a soft glow, but it is not water resistant (shellac

CUTTING RAISED PANELS ON THE TABLE SAW.

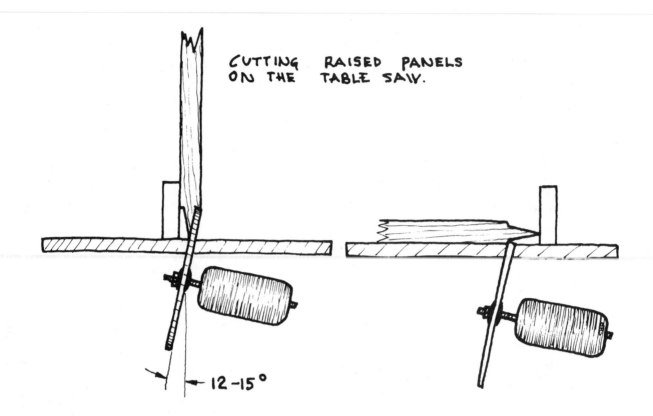

12-15°

HINGE UNDERCUT

SLIGHT ANGLE

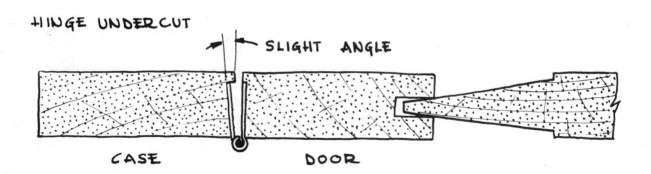

CASE   DOOR

ORDER OF ATTACHING MOULDING TO CASE

TOP VIEW

Applying stick shellac to a small imperfection in primary wood. This can be applied with a butane torch or hot knife.

Above: multiple passes with a table saw can rough in any moulding profile.

Below: by adjusting the angle of the diagonal wooden fence any cove contour can be cut in several passes with a dado blade.

turns chalky white if water-soaked). It takes considerable practice to apply this finish well.

Paint: The texture of buttermilk paint can be achieved by using a water-based acrylic latex paint. If applied directly on a wood surface, especially a softwood, the water in the paint will cause the grain to raise slightly, producing that old-looking texture. If a second coat is desired, sand lightly with 220 grit and apply the second coat. Again, all brush strokes should follow the wood's grain, especially on stiles and rails and drawer fronts. When the paint has hardened, in a day or two, it can be waxed with paste wax for a dull, deep sheen. If steel wool is used in applying the wax, the surface will appear slightly metallic and might enhance certain dark blues and greens. For earth tone colors this transluscence can be achieved by using a pigmented wax. A drop or two of universal colorant, sienna or umber, added to clear paste wax will work well. In buffing wax from a painted surface, a lint-free cloth should be used, and all excess wax should be removed. If a harder surface is desired, a painted finish can be varnished and steel-wooled following the method already described.

In working with Shaker forms it is unwise to overfinish. High-gloss, slick finishes might be appropriate to Chippendale or certain modern forms, but they don't seem appropriate to the simplicity that is inherent in these designs. Therefore I strongly recommend paint or rubbed oil as a finish. I also recommend that heavy staining be avoided. In time the sun and air will color the wood with a subtlety unmatched by anything that comes from a can.

Living with Shaker-Style Furniture

There is an art to living with these creations. They won't behave like Formica, but will swell and move from time to time. And they certainly will need occasional attention. Because we are dealing with solid wood, every effort should be made to place furnishings away from direct heat sources, such as radiators and, especially, hot air outlets. Also, large cases should not be pushed against baseboard heating elements since, in addition to producing split wood, this will result in inadequate heat circulation. If at all possible, the house should be equipped with a humidifier in winter to keep the humidity close to 50 percent. Remember, one reason two-hundred-year-old antiques have survived is that they were used in houses without central heating for the first one hundred and seventy five years. Extremes in temperature and humidity will wreak havoc with wood.

If your carefully finished table shows the marks of use, do not despair. A wear mark here, a slight burn there, a dent where one of the kids dropped a toy, surface scratches left by a pencil used in doing homework, the vestige of a telltale ring made two New Year's Eves ago—all these emboss a tabletop giving it warmth and charm and attesting to the life cycle of a family.

Hot linseed oil is applied and sanded when still wet with No. 500 wet and dry sandpaper for a satin smooth oil finish. High quality paste wax is applied after fifth coat of oil has dried.

Chapter 5

Measured Drawings

Two-Stepper

The Shakers built one-, two-, three-, and even four-steppers for use wherever
a shelf or pegboard or niche was too high to reach. This design began as a
copy of an old one, but it underwent dimensional changes to give it greater
stability. It makes an excellent library or kitchen steps and doubles as a
plant stand and even mini-bookcase. This is a good design for trying out
dovetails, and it assembles fairly easily.

MATERIALS: 7 board feet primary wood

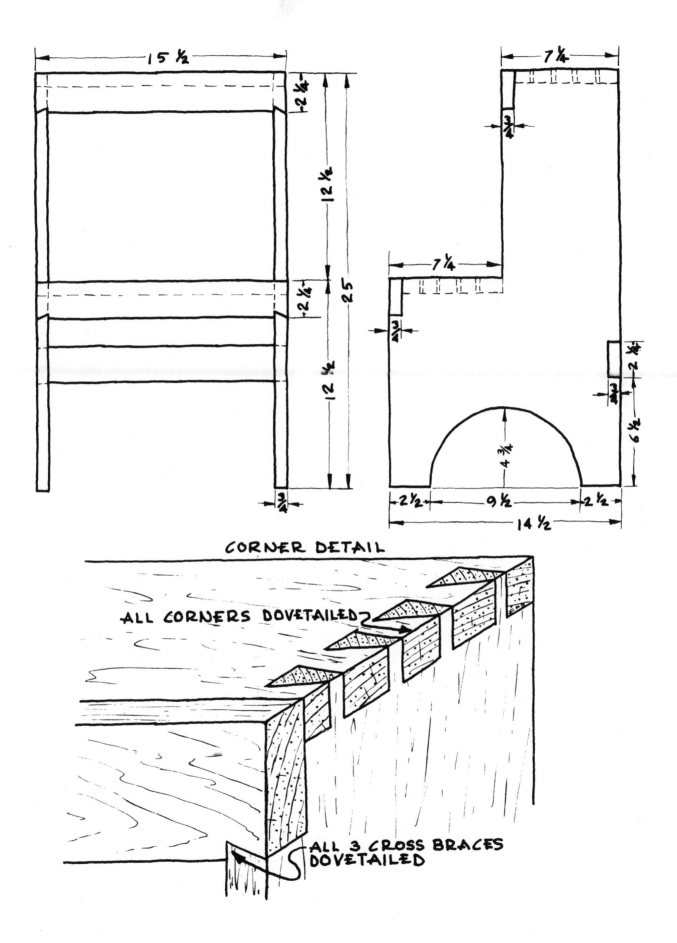

15 ½

2 ¼

12 ½

25

2 ¼

12 ½

¾

7 ¼

¾

7 ¼

¾

2 ¼

¾

6 ¼

4 ¾

2 ½

9 ½

2 ½

14 ½

CORNER DETAIL

ALL CORNERS DOVETAILED

ALL 3 CROSS BRACES
DOVETAILED

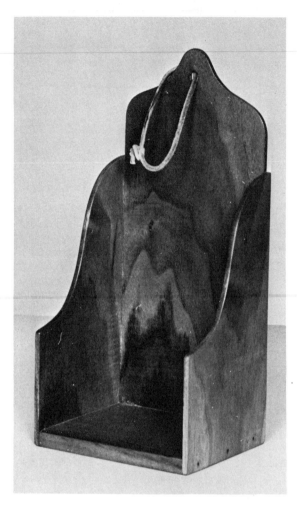

Candle Shelf

A number of these shelf designs were used by Shakers
to hold everything from candles to clay pipes to matches.
This one is ideal for a "hog scraper" candlestick.

MATERIALS: 1 board foot primary wood

Small Hanging Shelf

This form is found in the mirror hanger and can be adapted to a number
of uses for various kinds of hangers. It is a single 14-inch shelf that might
well hold a small potted flower.

MATERIALS: 1 board foot primary wood

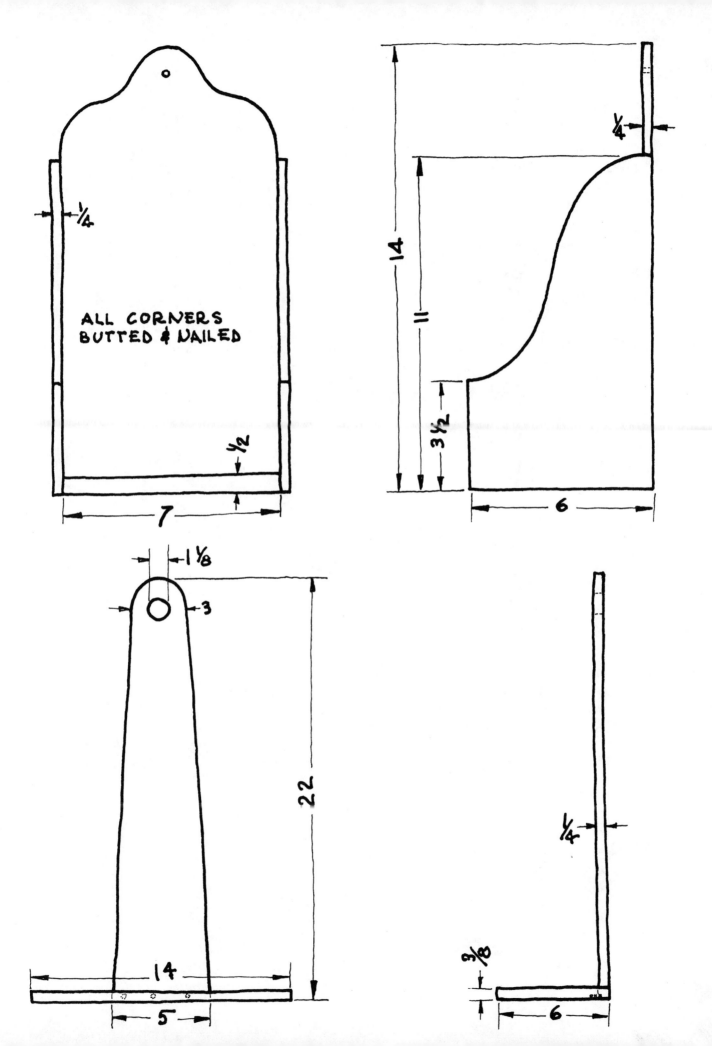

ALL CORNERS
BUTTED & NAILED

¼

½

7

14

¼

3½

6

1⅛

3

22

14

5

¼

⅜

6

Hanging Shelves

This simple set of shelves can be hung from a horizontal pegboard or mounted directly on a wall. It is simple to build and should provide an excellent opportunity to cut rabbet and dado joints.

MATERIALS: 6 board feet primary wood

Breadboard

One could build fifty breadboards and never build the same design twice. This model is taken from a sketch in a book by John Shea on Shaker museum classics. It can hang directly on a peg.

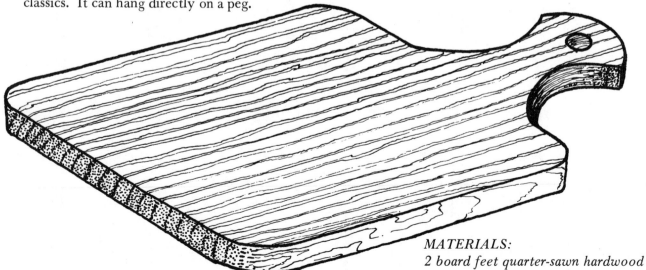

MATERIALS:
2 board feet quarter-sawn hardwood

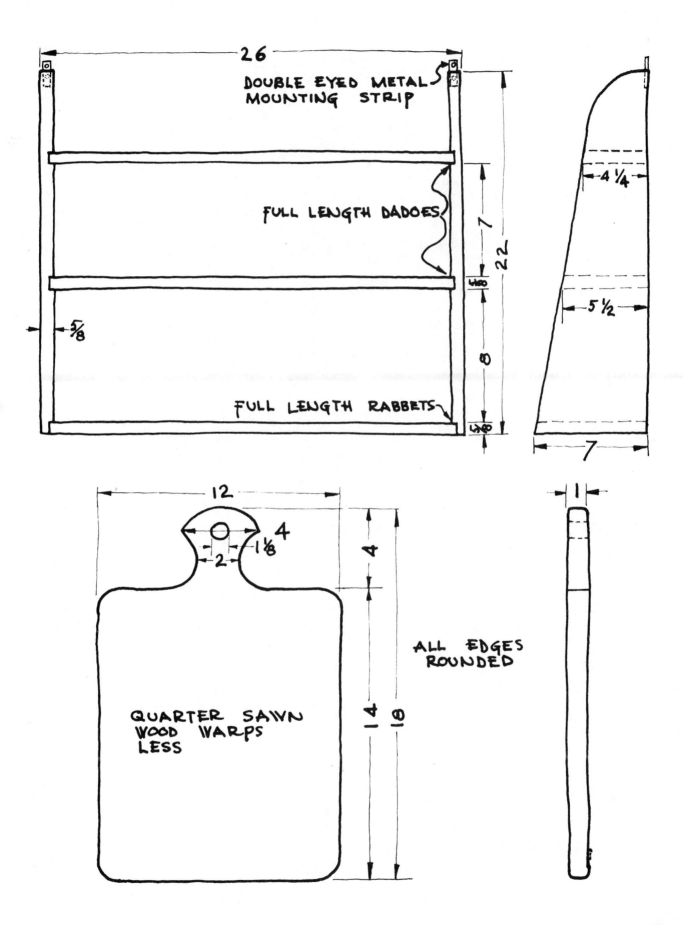

26

DOUBLE EYED METAL
MOUNTING STRIP

FULL LENGTH DADOES

22

7

4 1/4

5/8

5 1/2

8

FULL LENGTH RABBETS

7

12

1 1/8

4

2

QUARTER SAWN
WOOD WARPS
LESS

4

14

10

ALL EDGES
ROUNDED

1

Mirror

Designed to be suspended from the Shaker pegboard, this mirror has the added advantage of being adjustable. By lengthening or shortening the string in the hanger's slot the mirror can be focused down or up. For an unblemished reflection a plate glass mirror should be used. If single strength glass is used, add one-eighth inch to the wooden back. In fitting the back, leave space for swelling and shrinkage. The miter joint can be feathered, splined or lapped.

MATERIALS: 3 board feet primary wood,
14 3/8 " x 21 3/8 "
2 board feet secondary wood
plate glass mirror

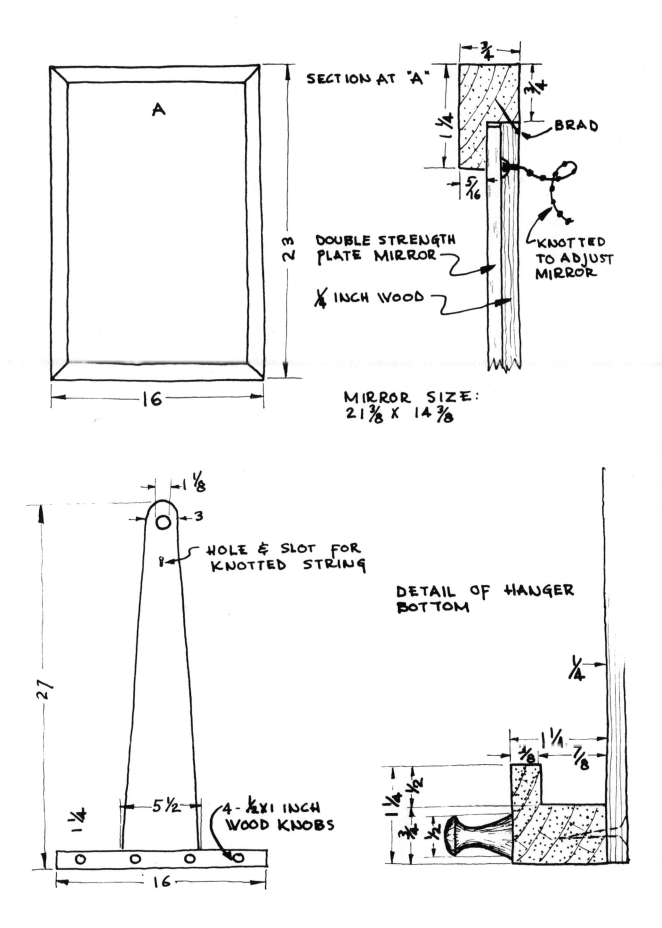

SECTION AT "A"

BRAD

KNOTTED TO ADJUST MIRROR

DOUBLE STRENGTH PLATE MIRROR

¼ INCH WOOD

MIRROR SIZE: 21⅜ X 14⅜

HOLE & SLOT FOR KNOTTED STRING

DETAIL OF HANGER BOTTOM

4 - ½ X 1 INCH WOOD KNOBS

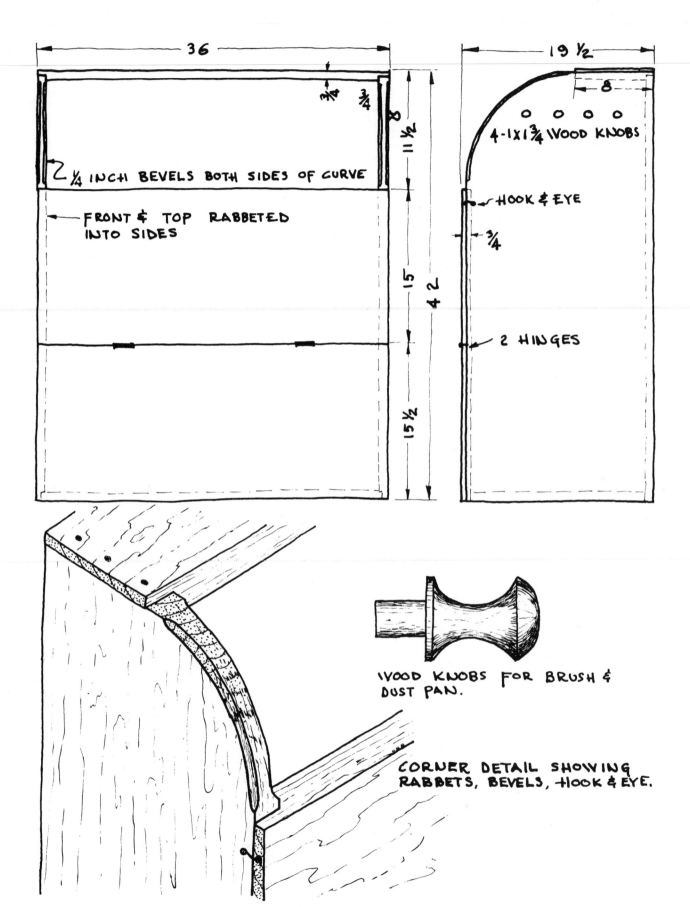

36

19 ½

¾   ¾

8

11 ½

¼ INCH BEVELS BOTH SIDES OF CURVE

FRONT & TOP RABBETED INTO SIDES

42

15

15 ½

4-1X1¾ WOOD KNOBS

HOOK & EYE

¾

2 HINGES

WOOD KNOBS FOR BRUSH & DUST PAN.

CORNER DETAIL SHOWING RABBETS, BEVELS, HOOK & EYE.

Wood Box

The clean lines of this box should make it at home wherever a wood stove or fireplace is used. The 15-inch hinged portion in front can be dropped when the level of the contents is sufficiently reduced, making access to the lower portion all the easier. This box is designed to take 18-inch or 36-inch logs. If your log dimension differs considerably, you may wish to alter the size of the box. No rabbet joints in this box should be glued since most of the grain runs at right angles.

MATERIALS: 36 board feet primary wood

Six-Board Chest

Americans of the nineteenth century would have called this a six-board chest; we say blanket box. Their term is more descriptive, since the box is literally made of six wide boards. Today, of course, these boards have to be glued up to achieve the necessary widths. No glue should be used at the joints in building the box. The grain directions are at right angles and the joint will only crack if glued. If pine is used, the end cleat should be made of hardwood.

MATERIALS: 45 board feet primary wood

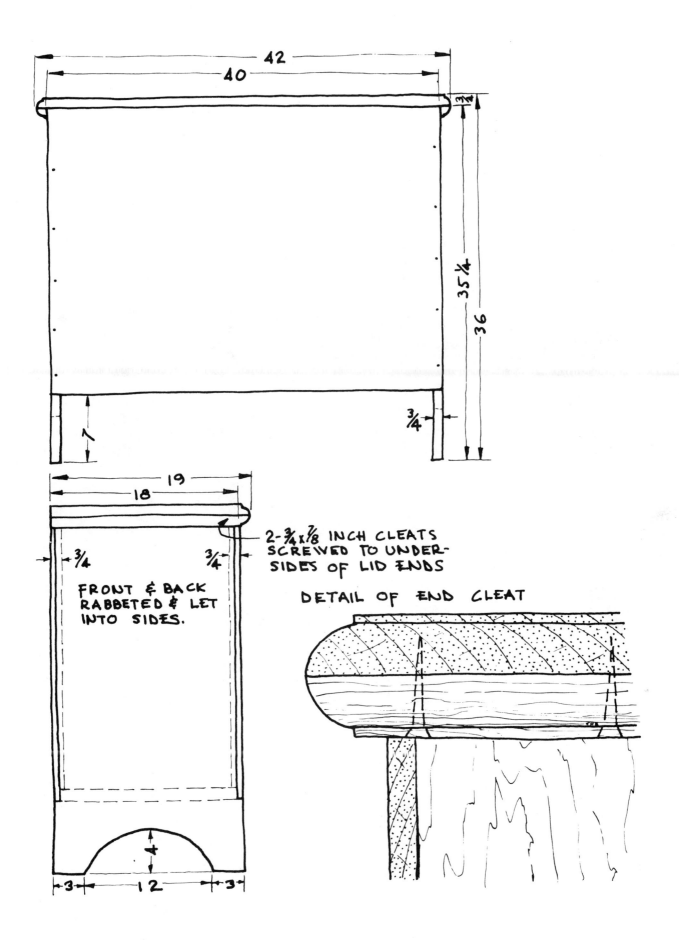

42

40

3/2

35 1/4

36

7

3/4

19

18

3/4   3/4

2-3/4 x 7/8 INCH CLEATS
SCREWED TO UNDER-
SIDES OF LID ENDS

FRONT & BACK
RABBETED & LET
INTO SIDES.

DETAIL OF END CLEAT

4

3   12   3

Common Bench

Strictly for utility, this bench offers no back support and is less than com-
fortable. Benches of this type were used at the dining table and often found
in workrooms. Ours is painted light blue and is placed out front next to the
walk in summer and used for holding potted geraniums in our bedroom in
winter. It can be reduced to a four-foot or five-foot length without upsetting the proportions.

MATERIALS: 13 board feet primary wood

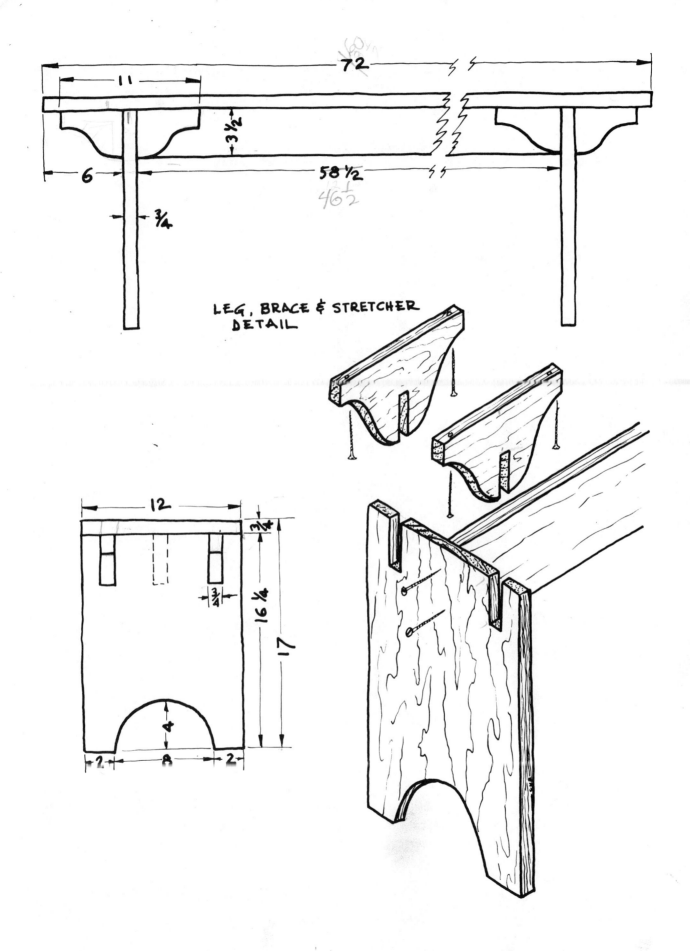

72

11

3½

6

58½

46½

¾

LEG, BRACE & STRETCHER
DETAIL

12

¾

¾

16¼

17

4

2   8   2

Large Round Stand

The feet on this stand extend slightly beyond the edge of the top to give it a stability not usually found in pedestal tables. For greatest strength, mark out the legs on the raw stock, so that the grain runs from one extreme point to another. The legs should be attached by careful gluing. When placing the top on the brace, make sure the grain of the top is at right angles to the grain of the brace.

MATERIALS: 7 board feet primary wood

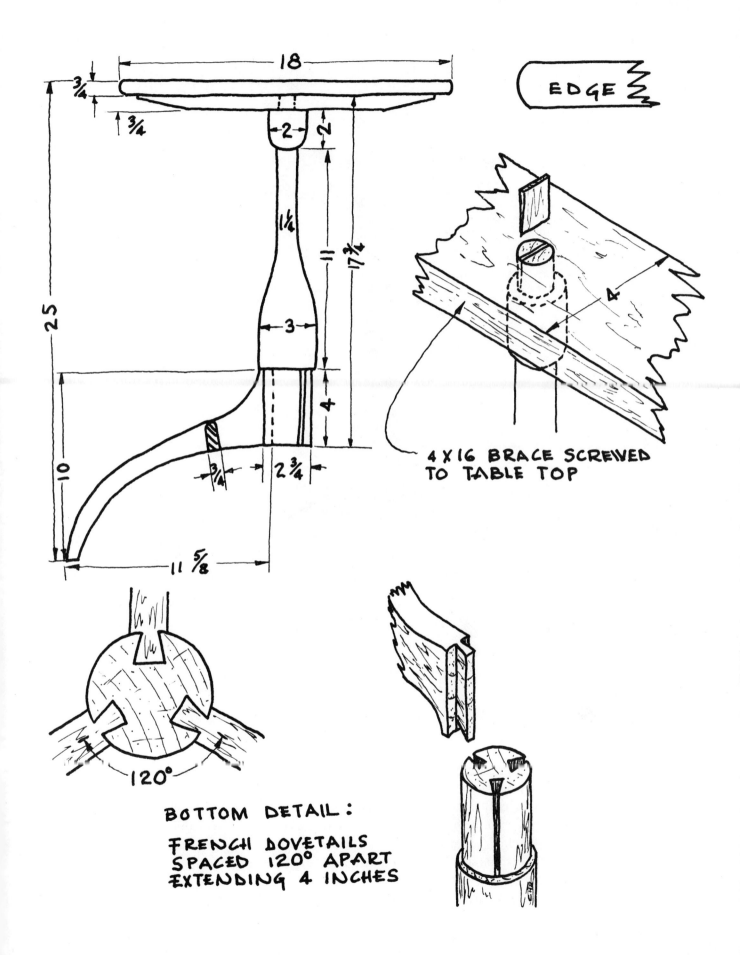

18

EDGE

3/4
3/4

3/4

2

2

1 1/4

17 3/4

3

25

11

4

10

3/4

2 3/4

11 5/8

4 X 16 BRACE SCREWED
TO TABLE TOP

4

120°

BOTTOM DETAIL:

FRENCH DOVETAILS
SPACED 120° APART
EXTENDING 4 INCHES

Small Round Stand

Everything about this pedestal table suggests twentieth-century authorship, yet one very much like it was built around 1830. Fitting the legs to the shaft is done by first cutting the male portion of the dovetail joint. This is then scribed onto the bottom of the pedestal and the slot is cut with back-saw and chisel. Proceed slowly to achieve a close fit. If a leg is too loose in the slot, a new one should be made with a slightly heavier dovetail.

MATERIALS: 6 board feet primary wood

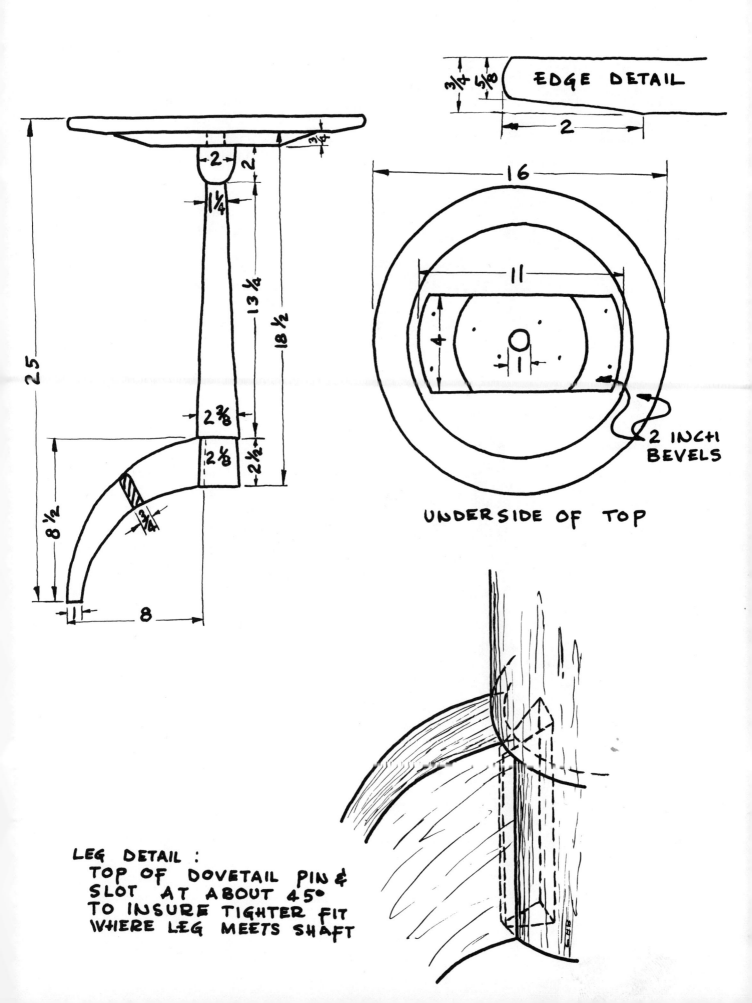

EDGE DETAIL

3/4   5/8

2

25

3/4

2

2

1¼

13¼

18½

2⅜

2⅛

2½

8½

3/4

8

16

11

4

1

2 INCH BEVELS

UNDERSIDE OF TOP

LEG DETAIL :
TOP OF DOVETAIL PIN &
SLOT AT ABOUT 45°
TO INSURE TIGHTER FIT
WHERE LEG MEETS SHAFT

Music Stand

Early Shaker doctrine was specific in banning the playing of and listening to instrumental music. Singing, however, was another story. Shaker songs, such as " 'Tis a Gift to be Simple," are now part of the folk repertoire of our country and are much appreciated. It is doubtful that the Shakers ever made a music stand, but if they had, it might well have looked like this. The base is patterned after the round stand but much larger in proportion. The stand itself has two adjustments and can be used from either a standing or sitting position. A set of these might be perfect for a chamber ensemble.

The pedestal is made by gluing together two pieces of stock into which have been cut one-inch "V" grooves. When together, the two "V" grooves form a square slot which accommodates the shaft. Tapered plugs are inserted in both ends to receive the lathe stocks for turning. At its widest point the pedestal should not exceed 2¾ inches.

MATERIALS: 8 board feet primary
wood
White ash spindles
Rock maple pins

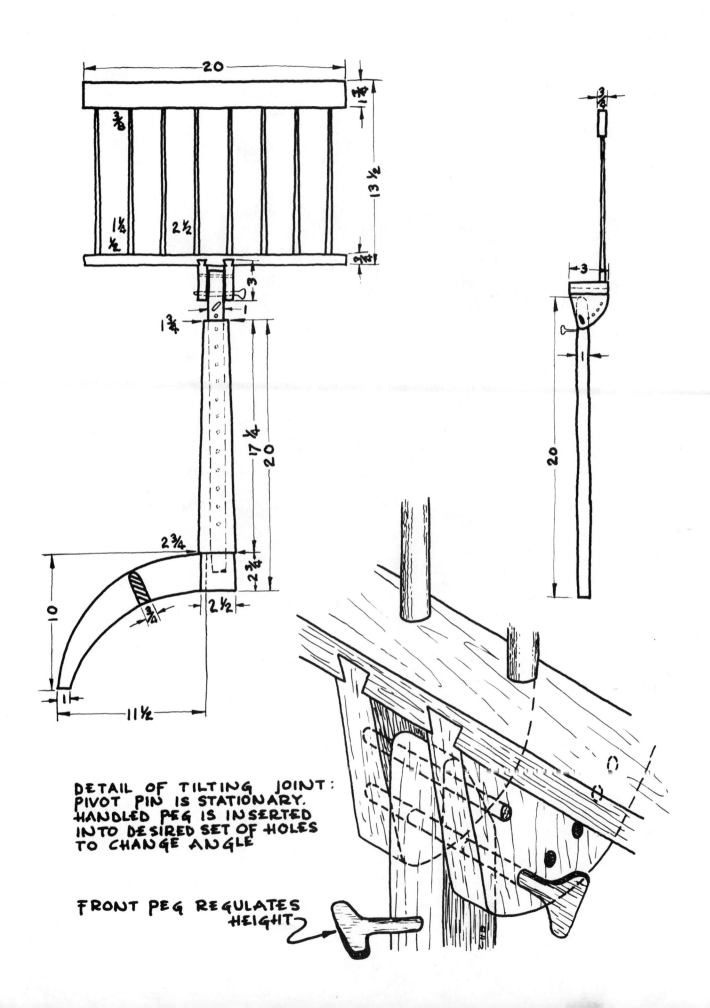

20

⅜

1¾

13 ½

¾

2½

1⅛

½

3

1¾

17¼

20

2¾

2¾

10

¾

2½

1

11½

¾

3

20

DETAIL OF TILTING JOINT:
PIVOT PIN IS STATIONARY.
HANDLED PEG IS INSERTED
INTO DESIRED SET OF HOLES
TO CHANGE ANGLE

FRONT PEG REGULATES
HEIGHT

Hanging Cupboard

This design started out half the size and with a single board door. Improvements have resulted in this set of shelves that will be useful in the bathroom or in the kitchen to hold anything from soap to soup. It, too, can be hung on a pegboard or simply on a finish nail almost any place.

MATERIALS: 9 board feet primary wood

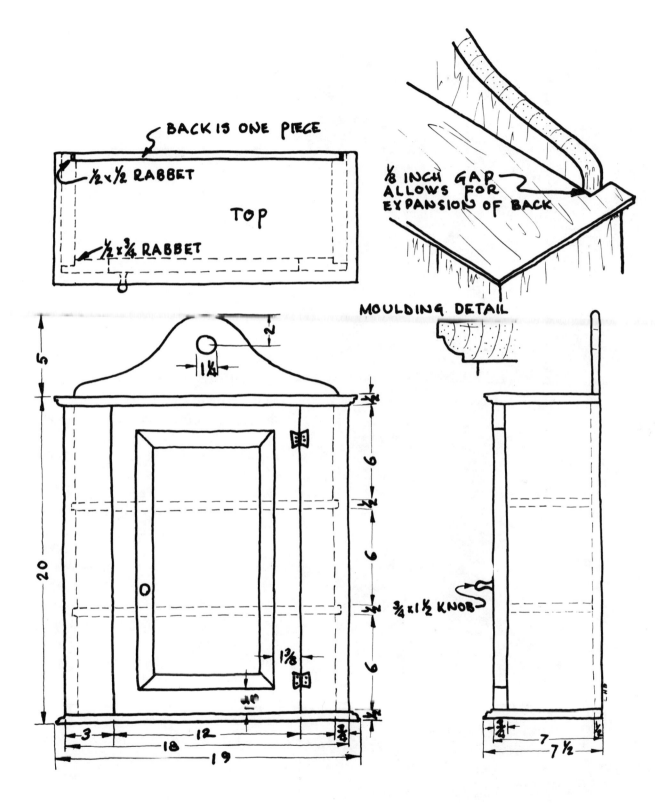

BACK IS ONE PIECE

½ x ½ RABBET

TOP

½ x ¾ RABBET

⅛ INCH GAP
ALLOWS FOR
EXPANSION OF BACK

MOULDING DETAIL

BACK IS ONE PIECE

5

20

2

1¼

½

6

4½

6

½

6

½

1⅜

¾ x 1½ KNOB

3

12

18

¾

19

¾

7

7½

½

Revolving Stool

To the Shakers a stool that turned on a pedestal was called a revolver, a term hardly appropriate today. This stool rests on a base that consists of two identical legs which are attached with a lap joint, through which the round base of the pedestal is passed. On top of the pedestal, a 2-inch length of 1 1/2-inch steel pipe is forced. The chair back is made by slicing a board into 1/8 inch x 3/4 inch x 22 inch strips, which are then glued together in a wooden press to achieve the crescent shape. After it has hardened, the back is shaped with a rasp and file. The 1/4-inch diameter steel spindles are cold-formed, driven into 15/64-inch holes bored into the seat and back and are held in place by friction and their mutual antagonism. The stool makes a surprisingly strong seat.

MATERIALS: 9 board feet primary wood
10 lineal feet 1/4" soft steel rod
8 inches, 1/2" steel rod
1 half-inch ball bearing
1 8" x 1/8" steel plate

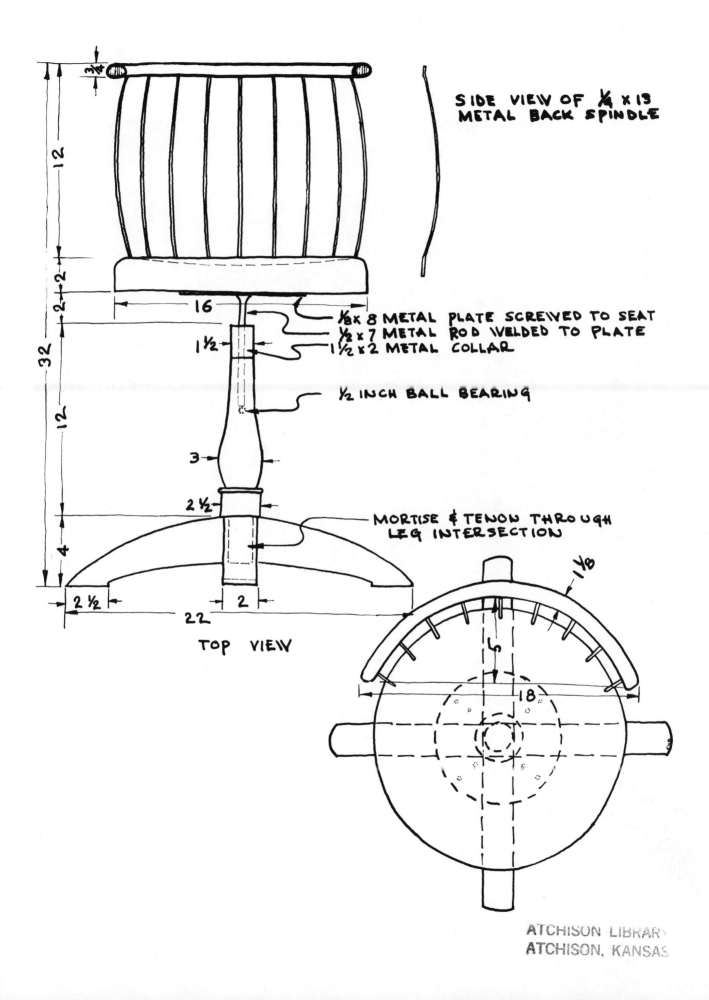

SIDE VIEW OF ⅛ × 13 METAL BACK SPINDLE

¾

12

16

2
2
2
32

⅛ × 8 METAL PLATE SCREWED TO SEAT
½ × 7 METAL ROD WELDED TO PLATE
1½ × 2 METAL COLLAR

1½

½ INCH BALL BEARING

12

3

2½

MORTISE & TENON THROUGH LEG INTERSECTION

4

2½

2

22

TOP VIEW

1⅛

5

18

Four-Door Side Chest

Where more free-standing cupboard space and less drawer space are required, this low chest may well be the answer. In an apartment or other setting having limited space this makes a superb side piece. If desired, the interior shelf can be made adjustable by adding extra cleats.

MATERIALS: 36 board feet primary wood
25 board feet primary wood

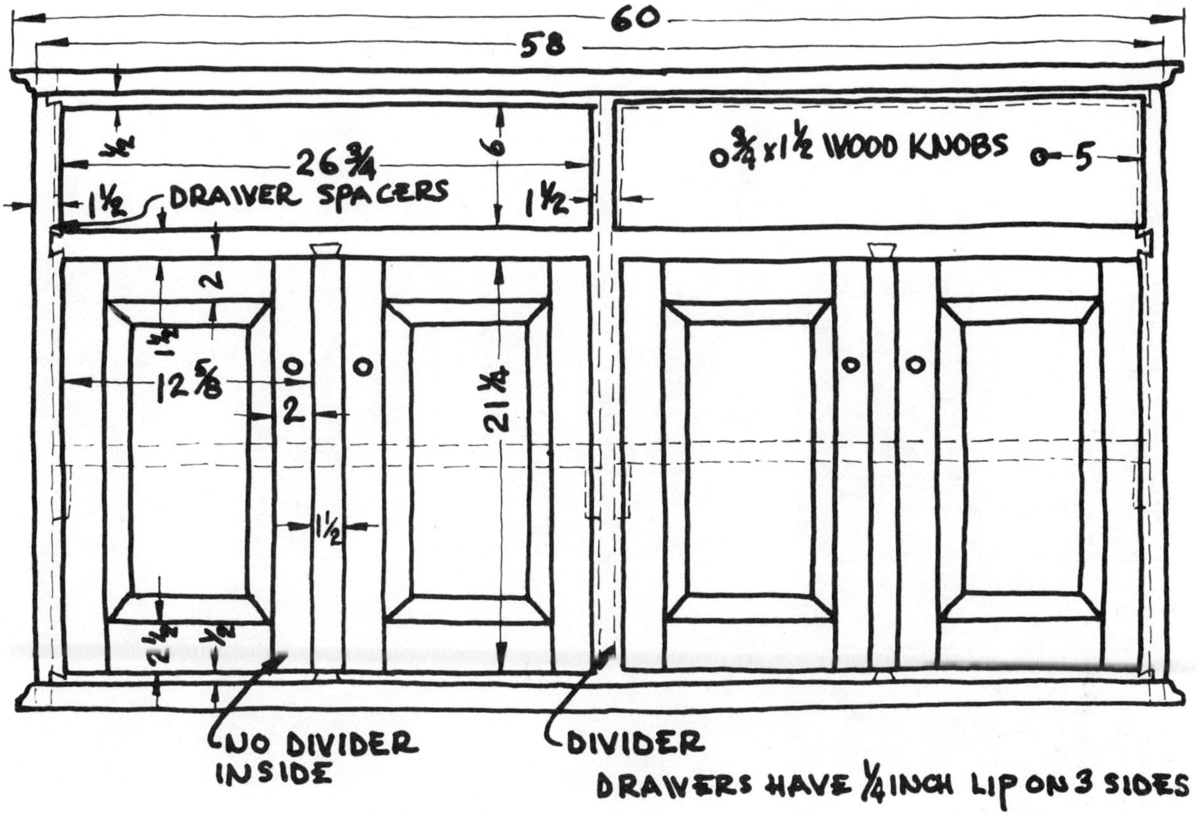
60
58
1/4
26 3/4
6
1 1/2
DRAWER SPACERS
1 1/2
0 3/4 x 1 1/2 WOOD KNOBS
5
2
12 5/8
2
21 1/4
1 1/2
2 1/4
NO DIVIDER INSIDE
DIVIDER
DRAWERS HAVE 1/4 INCH LIP ON 3 SIDES

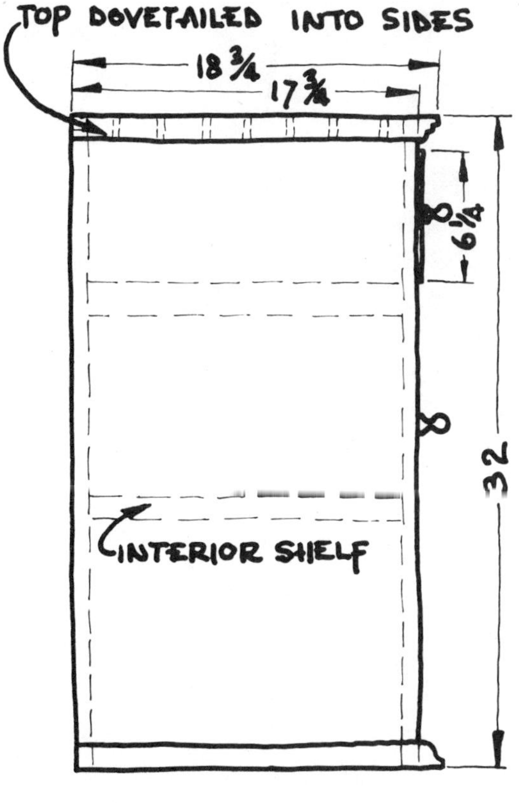
TOP DOVETAILED INTO SIDES
18 3/4
17 3/4
6 1/4
32
INTERIOR SHELF

DOOR FRAME & PANEL DETAIL

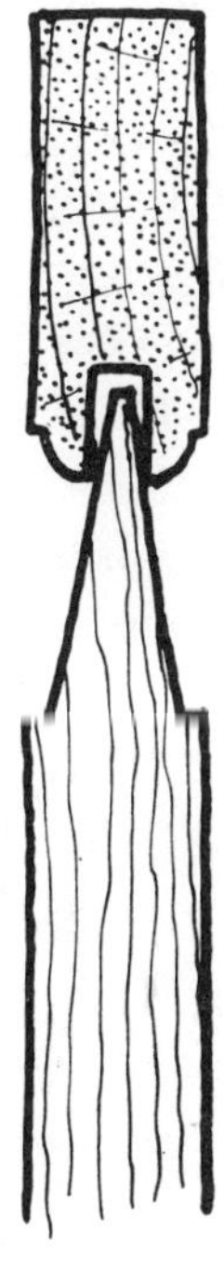

BOTTOM MOULDING

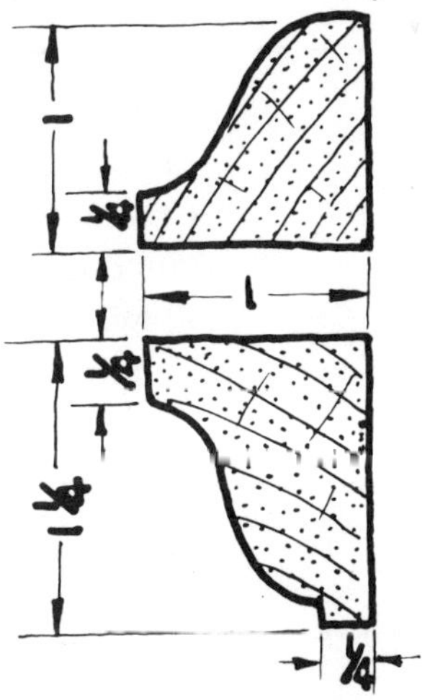
1
1/4
1
1/4
1 1/4
1/4

TOP MOULDING

Six-Drawer Side Chest

What we call the side chest had its origin in the work counter of a weaving room in New Lebanon. By slightly changing a few dimensions this six-drawer chest emerged. Since these dimensions resulted in such a useful and usually satisfying cabinet space, we decided to experiment with different drawer configurations and even added a door. Hence these three side chest combinations. If relatively deep drawer space is required, then the six-drawer side chest is the answer. Unlike the standing chests these cases require face stiles and rails to be applied to the carcass.

MATERIALS:

36 board feet primary wood
38 board feet secondary wood

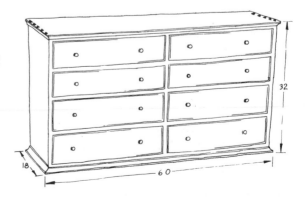

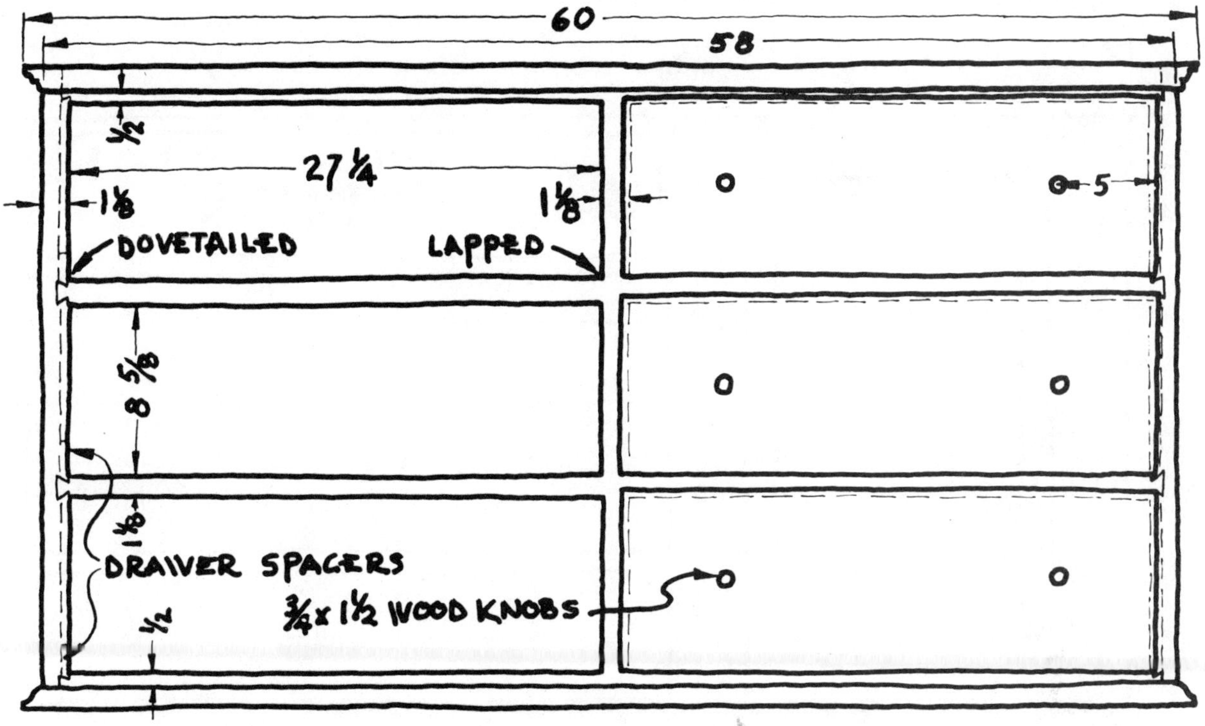
60
58
1/2
27 1/4
1 1/8
1 1/8
DOVETAILED
LAPPED
5
8 5/8
1 1/8
DRAWER SPACERS
3/4 x 1 1/2 WOOD KNOBS
1/2

ALL DRAWERS HAVE 1/4 INCH LIP ON 3 SIDES

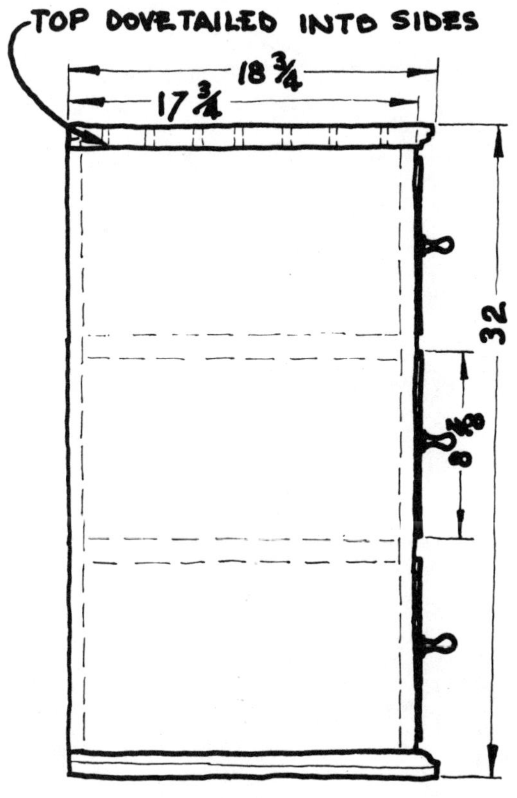
TOP DOVETAILED INTO SIDES
18 3/4
17 3/4
32
8 5/8

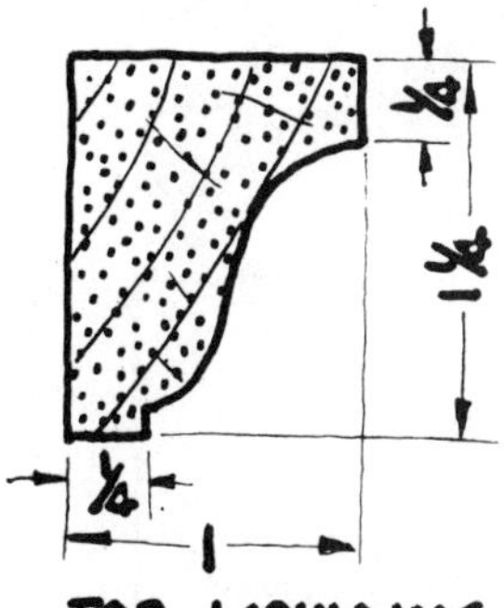
1/4
1 1/4
1/4
1

TOP MOULDING

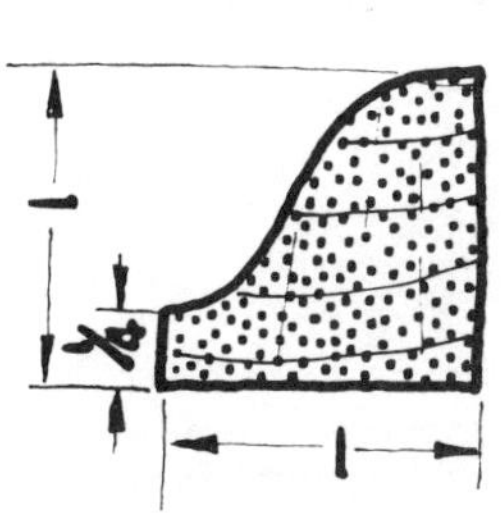
1
1/4
1

BOTTOM MOULDING

TOP CORNER SHOWING DOVETAILS

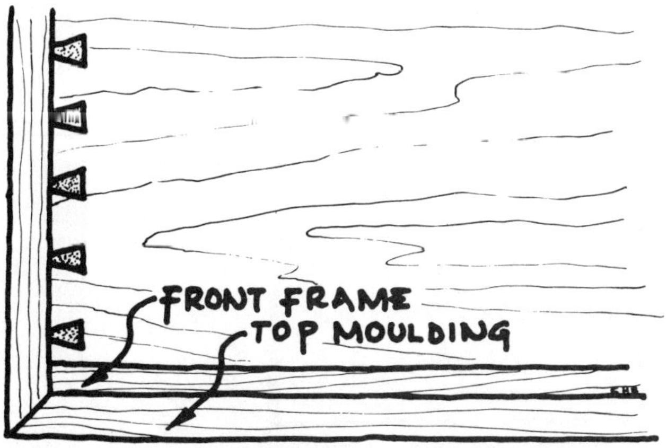
FRONT FRAME
TOP MOULDING

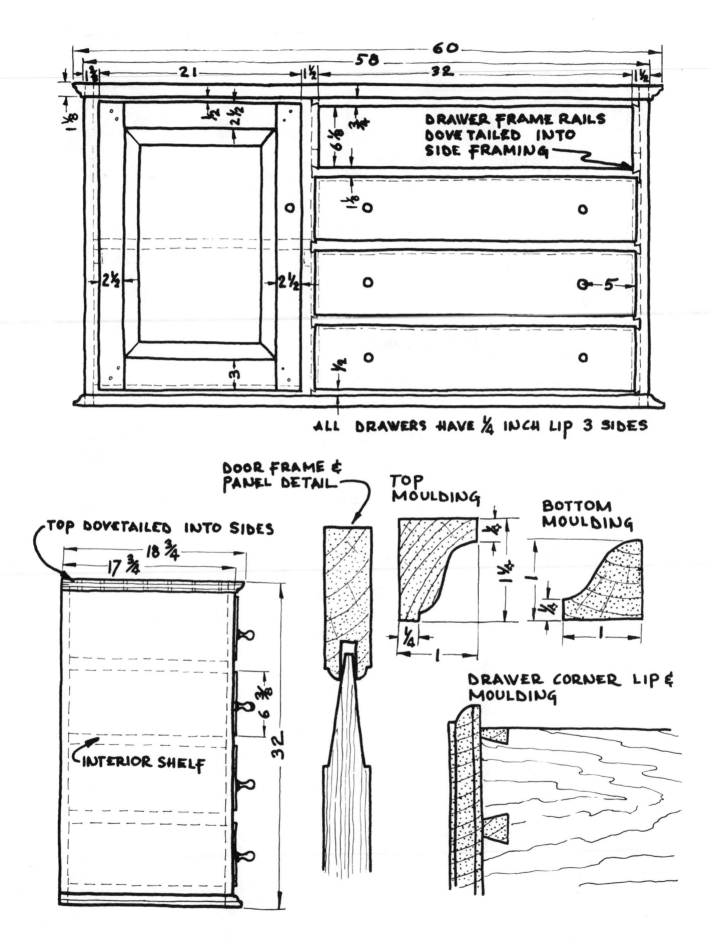

60
58
21
1½
32
1½
1⅛
1⅝
½
2½
¾
6⅝

DRAWER FRAME RAILS DOVETAILED INTO SIDE FRAMING

1⅛

2⅛
2½
5

3
½

ALL DRAWERS HAVE ¼ INCH LIP 3 SIDES

DOOR FRAME & PANEL DETAIL
TOP MOULDING
BOTTOM MOULDING

TOP DOVETAILED INTO SIDES
18¾
17¾

6⅜
32

INTERIOR SHELF

⅛
1¼
¼
1

1
½
1

DRAWER CORNER LIP & MOULDING

Four-Drawer Side Chest

When used as a sideboard in a dining room, the four-drawer side chest
provides ample space for storing tablecloths, napkins, flatware of all sorts,
and still provides space for storing fairly tall objects which would not
comfortably fit in a drawer. We know of several that are used to house
beverage bottles, mixers, and sundry items. As a bedroom chest the uses
are limitless. Hats, shoes, even ski boots can go into the cupboard portion.

MATERIALS: 36 board feet primary wood
38 board feet secondary wood

Pewter Cupboard

No doubt eyebrows will rise because this pewter cupboard is pictured in a book on Shaker style. Strictly speaking, it does not belong in this genre since it is designed to display china, pewter, glassware, and "display" was categorically disapproved of in Shaker doctrine. Nevertheless, we encourage this slight frivolity and include the design anyway. A cupboard very much like this is included in the Sturbridge collection and another in Springfield, Massachusetts. The "C" scroll seems to have been popular with the early New Englanders and has found a delightful expression in this piece. The cupboard door is shown in the raised panel and also the simple board and batten and is entirely optional. This piece looks best in dark red, blue, or green and also in natural pine or cherry. If you haven't enough wide boards to build the back in three pieces, glue them up so as to use only two beaded joints. Also, note the use of butterfly hinges and base moulding on the pine cupboard.

MATERIALS: 65 board feet primary wood

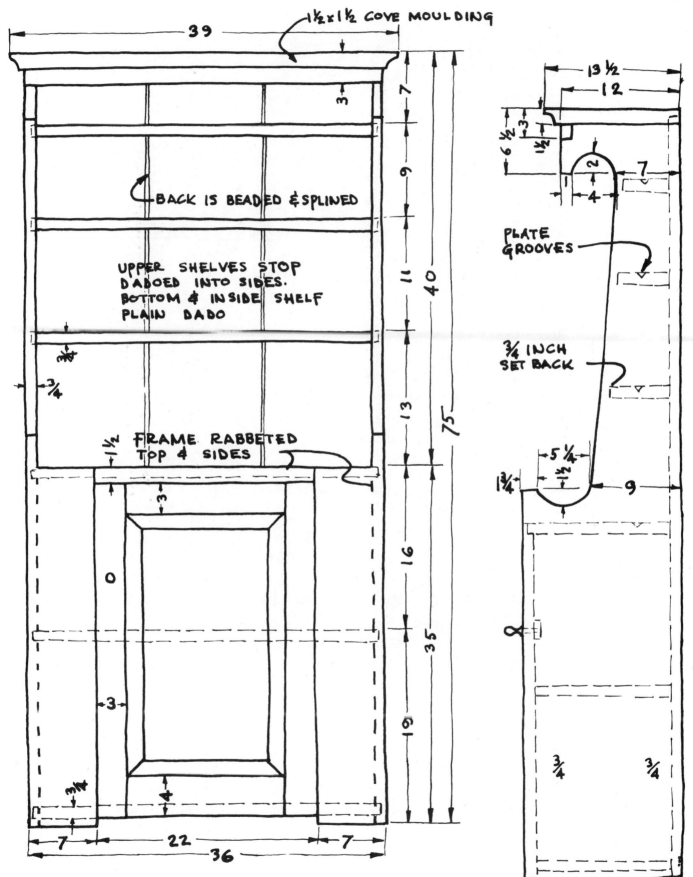

1½ x 1½ COVE MOULDING

39

7

3

BACK IS BEADED & SPLINED

9

UPPER SHELVES STOP
DADOED INTO SIDES.
BOTTOM & INSIDE SHELF
PLAIN DADO

11

40

75

¾

13

3

1½ FRAME RABBETED
TOP & SIDES

3

16

0

35

3

19

4

¾

7

22

7

36

13½

12

6½ 3
1½

2

4

7

PLATE
GROOVES

¾ INCH
SET BACK

9

5¼
½

1¾

16

Dr. White's Chest

If I could only have one piece of furniture to hold all my belongings, this would be my choice. Between the seven drawers and cupboard shelves there is adequate space to house everything I could ever need. If it couldn't fit in Dr. White's Chest, I wouldn't need it. This is the heaviest piece in the collection. We build this chest with a hidden compartment — but if we drew it, then it would no longer be hidden.

MATERIALS: 50 board feet primary wood
50 board feet secondary wood

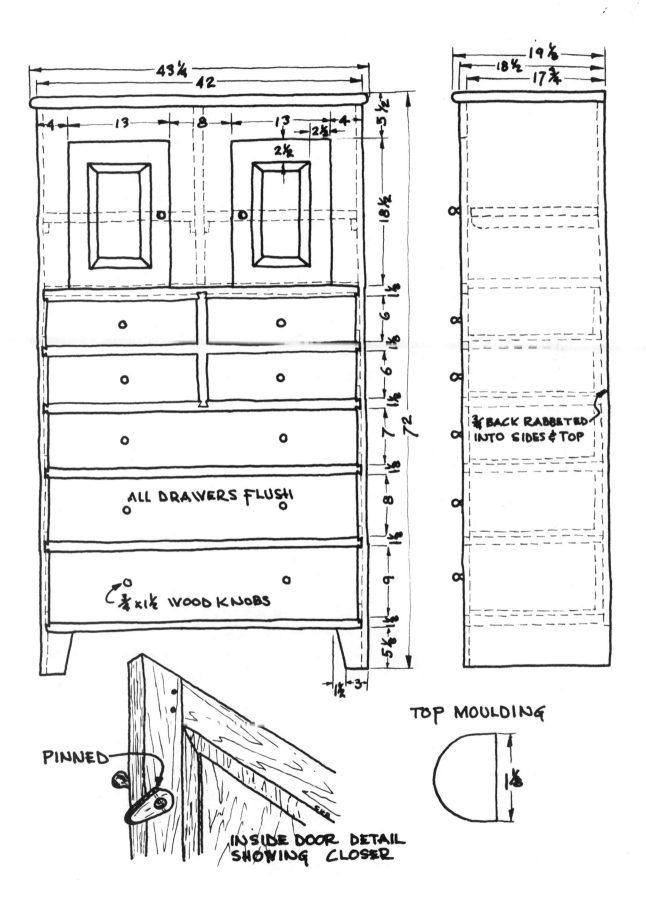

ALL DRAWERS FLUSH

¾ x 1½ WOOD KNOBS

¾ BACK RABBETED INTO SIDES & TOP

PINNED

INSIDE DOOR DETAIL
SHOWING CLOSER

TOP MOULDING

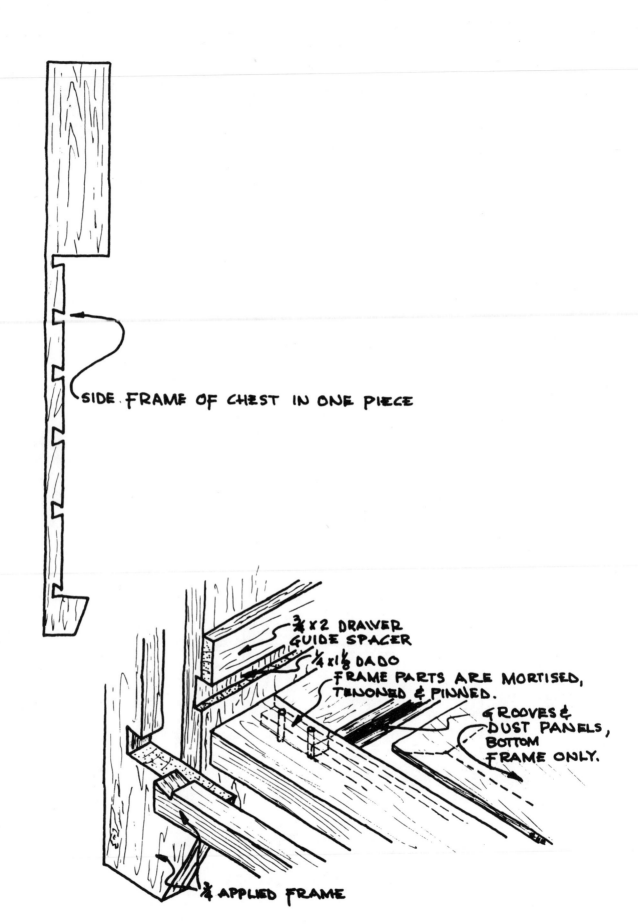

SIDE FRAME OF CHEST IN ONE PIECE

¾ x 2 DRAWER
GUIDE SPACER

¼ x 1⅛ DADO

FRAME PARTS ARE MORTISED,
TENONED & PINNED.

GROOVES &
DUST PANELS,
BOTTOM
FRAME ONLY.

¾ APPLIED FRAME

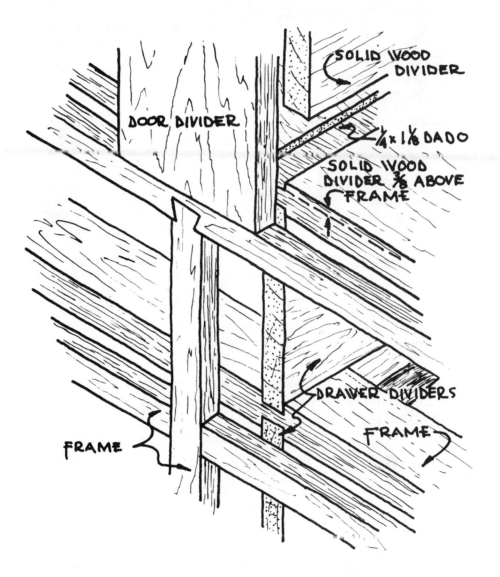

SOLID WOOD
DIVIDER

DOOR DIVIDER

1/4 x 1 1/8 DADO

SOLID WOOD
DIVIDER 3/8 ABOVE
FRAME

DRAWER DIVIDERS

FRAME

FRAME

Trestle Table

The oldest known American-made table in the United States is a one-board, sixteen-inch-wide trestle table now housed in the American Wing of the Metropolitan Museum in New York. This concept of a removable board on a double or triple pedestal base has its origin in medieval times. The trestle dining table is clearly one of the oldest and simplest furniture forms in existence. It was the Shakers who, with a number of trestle designs, brought this form to the level of an art. Ours, a composite of several designs, has proven popular in both the dining room and the kitchen. The table can be extended to eight feet by adding two feet to the top and center stretcher. If more width is needed, as much as three or four inches can be added, but no more, since the brace and leg components cannot take too great a stress. Furthermore, the table looks best with a long, slender top.

MATERIALS: 42 board feet primary wood

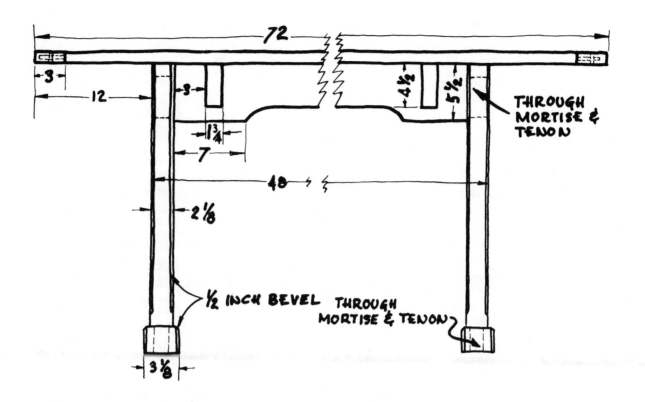

72

3

12

3

1¾

7

4½

5½

THROUGH
MORTISE &
TENON

48

2⅛

½ INCH BEVEL THROUGH
MORTISE & TENON

3⅛

TRESTLE & BRACE DETAIL

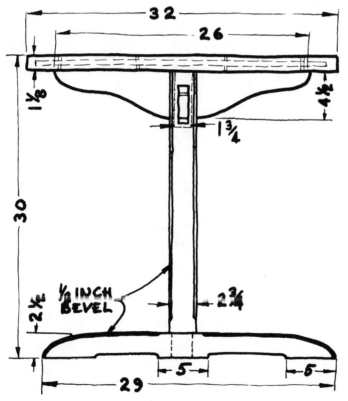

32

26

1⅛

4½

1¾

30

½ INCH
BEVEL

2¾

2½

5

5

29

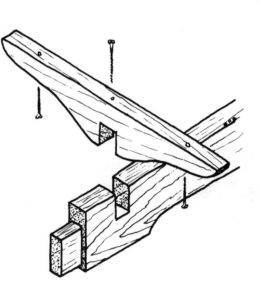

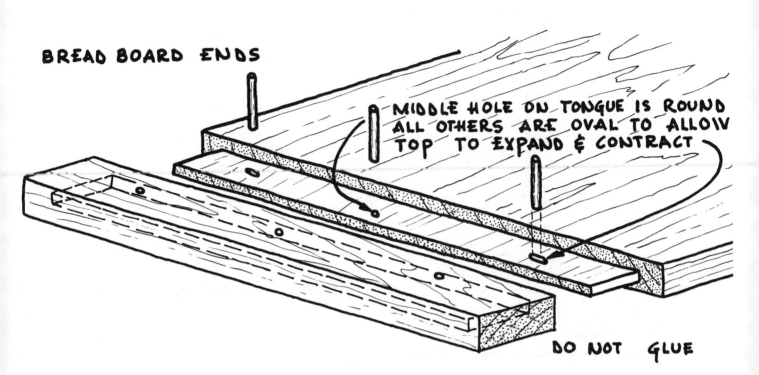

BREAD BOARD ENDS

MIDDLE HOLE ON TONGUE IS ROUND ALL OTHERS ARE OVAL TO ALLOW TOP TO EXPAND & CONTRACT

DO NOT GLUE

Trestle Table Mortise and Tenon Options

A six-foot trestle table can be moved from room to room and up and down stairs with little effort. It can be made in one monolithic form using a through mortise and tenon with glue and wedges at the upper leg joint. If, however, one extends the table to eight feet, or wishes greater mobility, removable legs can be made by using either the keyed tenon or a pair of common bed bolts. If properly done, all three systems will result in a stable base which should not tip or rock with reasonable use.

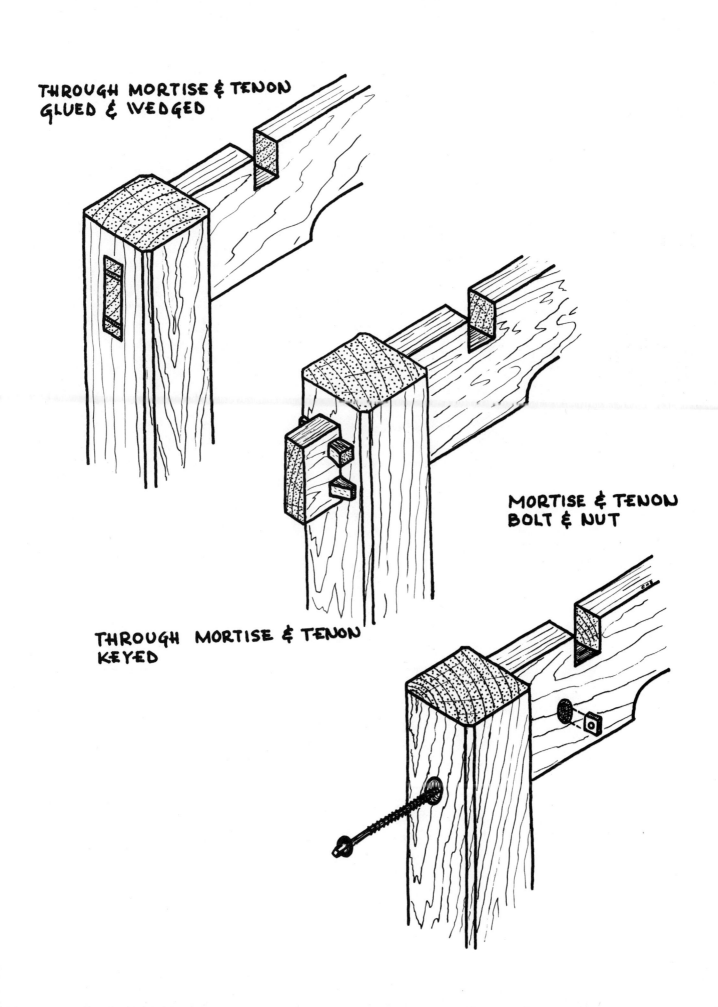

THROUGH MORTISE & TENON
GLUED & WEDGED

MORTISE & TENON
BOLT & NUT

THROUGH MORTISE & TENON
KEYED

Coffee Table

There were no low coffee tables in the eighteenth and nineteenth centuries. The tea tables that did exist were quite high and not intended for use in front of a couch or in the center of a living room conversation area. Why this idea had to wait until the twentieth century I do not know, but the fact is the coffee table is a strictly modern notion. This design is a miniature trestle table altogether at home as a low table for serving coffee, cheese, or whatever. If it is to be placed in front of an extremely low contemporary couch, it might be lowered an inch or two. Conversely, if the couch is quite high, an inch can be added. The chairs with the coffee table are not in the Shaker style, but are pictured to show the relative size of the table.

MATERIALS: 24 board feet primary wood

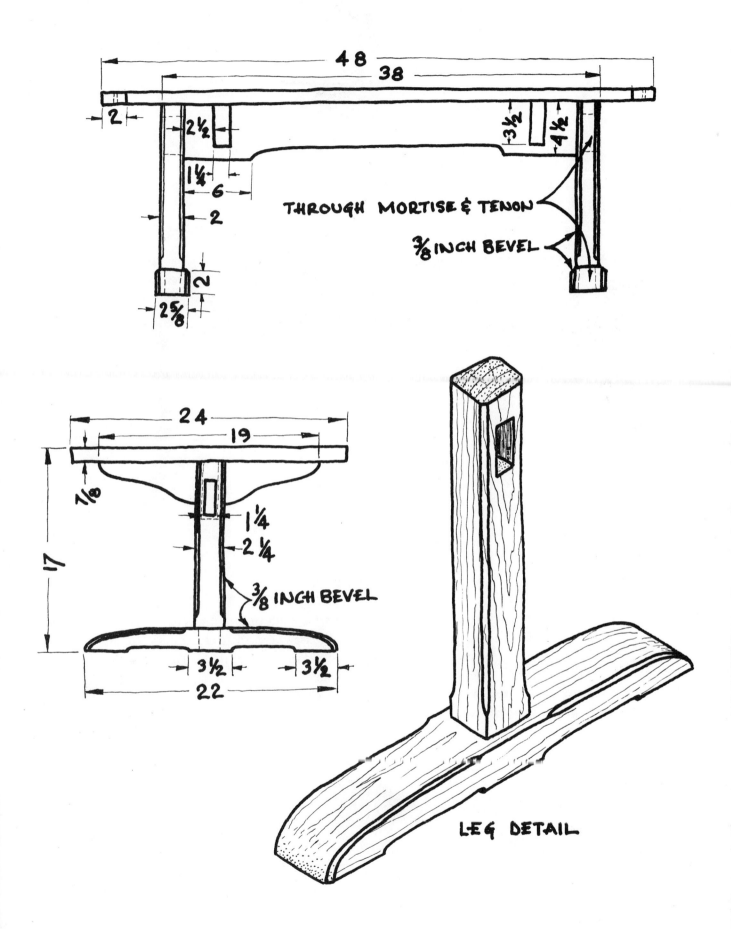

48

38

2

2½

3½

4½

1¼

6

2

THROUGH MORTISE & TENON

⅜ INCH BEVEL

2

2⅝

24

19

7⅛

17

1¼

2¼

⅜ INCH BEVEL

3½

3½

22

LEG DETAIL

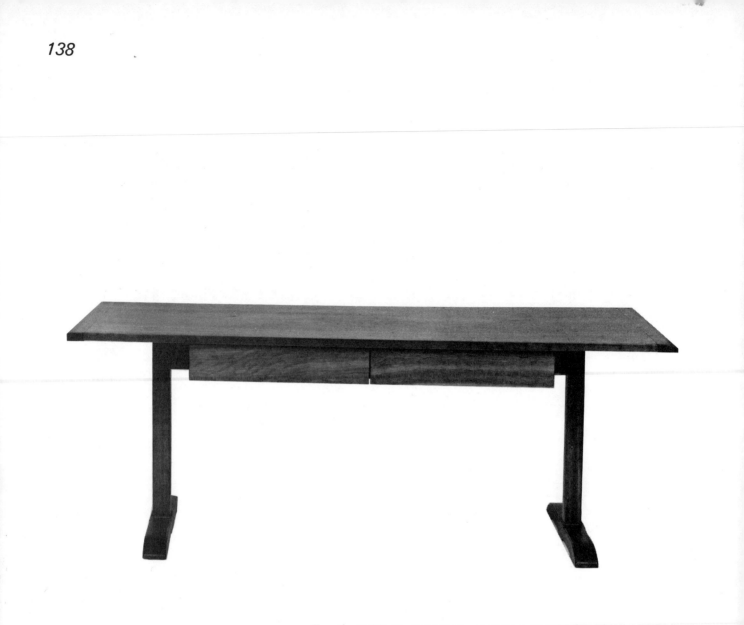

Trestle Table Desk

A desk need not be a massive, cumbersome affair with tiers of drawers.
If storage can be arranged in filing cabinets or elsewhere, the trestle table
form makes a light, informal, totally useful working table or desk. The two
shallow drawers offer sufficient room for a small assortment of paper and
writing materials. We use this table in our kitchen where the drawers house
napkins and several sets of place mats.

MATERIALS: 42 board feet primary wood
16 board feet secondary wood

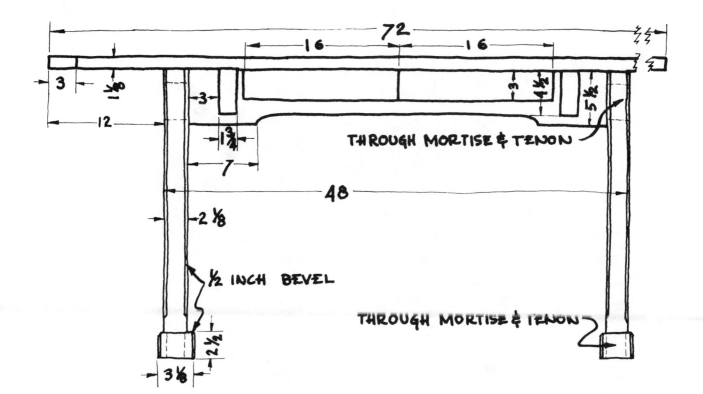

72

16 16

3

12

3

THROUGH MORTISE & TENON

3 4½ 5½

1¾

7

48

2⅛

½ INCH BEVEL

THROUGH MORTISE & TENON

2½

3⅛

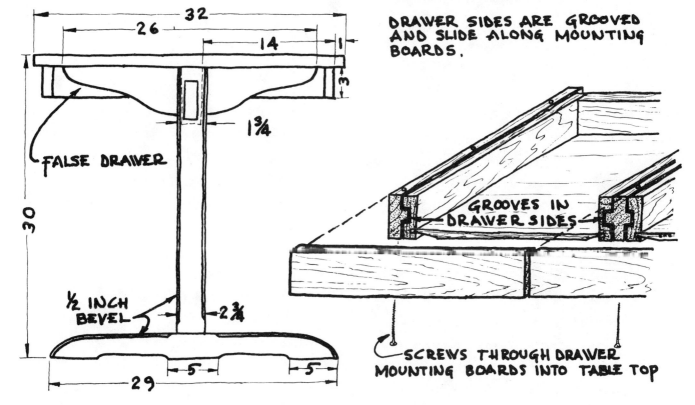

32

26

14 1

3

FALSE DRAWER

1¾

30

½ INCH
BEVEL

2¾

29

5 5

DRAWER DETAIL:

DRAWER SIDES ARE GROOVED
AND SLIDE ALONG MOUNTING
BOARDS.

GROOVES IN
DRAWER SIDES

SCREWS THROUGH DRAWER
MOUNTING BOARDS INTO TABLE TOP

140

Side Stand

The graceful tapered leg terminating in a 5/8-inch tip gives this table
a lightness quite remarkable. It makes a perfect reading stand or a useful
table next to a bed. This project offers a good exercise in the use of
mortise and tenon as well as drawer construction.

MATERIALS: 8 board feet primary wood

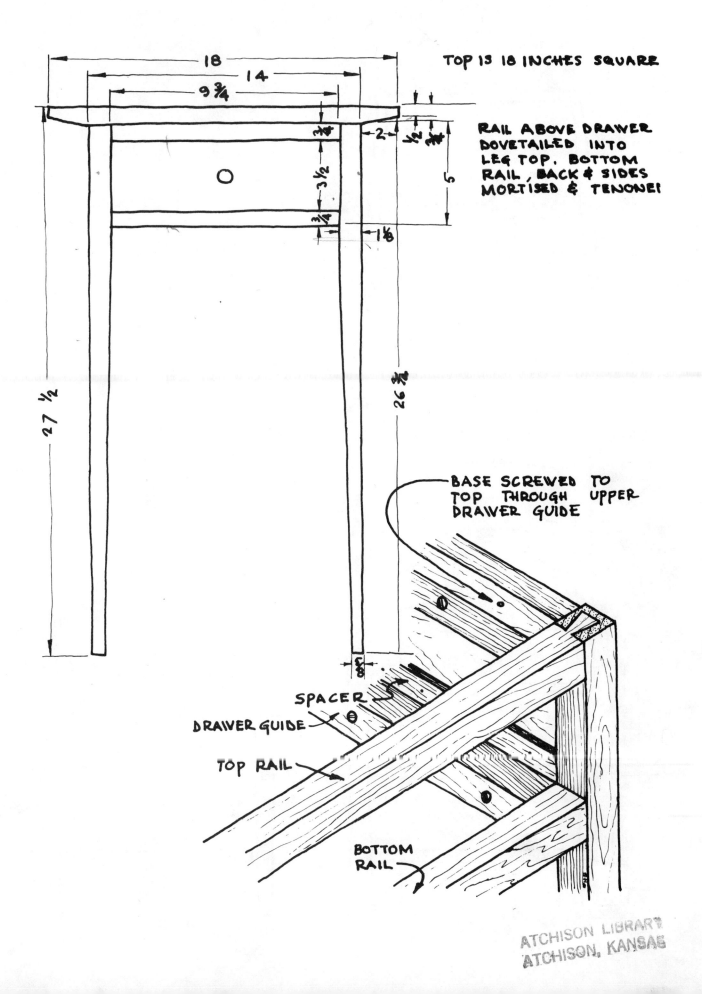

18

14

9¾

3¼

2

3½

3/4

1⅛

½

3¼

5

26¾

27½

TOP IS 18 INCHES SQUARE

RAIL ABOVE DRAWER
DOVETAILED INTO
LEG TOP. BOTTOM
RAIL, BACK & SIDES
MORTISED & TENONED

BASE SCREWED TO
TOP THROUGH UPPER
DRAWER GUIDE

5/8

SPACER

DRAWER GUIDE

TOP RAIL

BOTTOM
RAIL

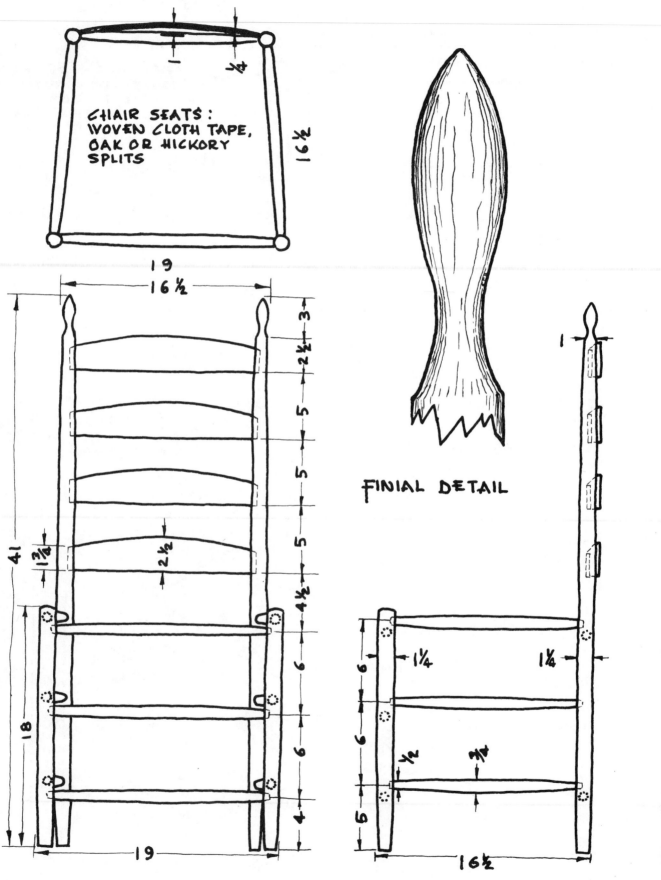

CHAIR SEATS:
WOVEN CLOTH TAPE,
OAK OR HICKORY
SPLITS

¼

16½

19

16½

3

2½

5

5

5

5

4½

6

6

4

1¾

2½

41

18

19

FINIAL DETAIL

1

6

6

6

9

1¼

1¼

½

¾

16½

Four-Slat Ladderback Chair

For lightness 1¼ inch hardwood dowels are used in the legs. To turn the back legs, chuck a 42-inch length into a lathe and taper one end from about 18 inches in toward the end and turn the finial (see full-size detail). When the legs are turned, cut four 1¾ inch slots in line entering about ¾ inch. Front and rear legs are then bored for ½-inch stretchers at a depth of 5/8 inches. The back slats are cut to shape and steamed in a steambox and bent on a clamping jig using two C-clamps. When dry, they are fitted to the slots in the rear legs. All sockets are glued and pegged with 1/8-inch dowels.

Chair seats can be made of cloth fabric, splint, or rush. These chairs are pictured in a kind of splint installed for us at the Maine Institution for the Blind in Portland. Chair seat fabric tape and directions for weaving can be ordered from Shaker Workshops, Concord, Massachusetts.

MATERIALS: 3 48" x 1¼" dowels
6 36" x ¾" dowels
1 board foot hardwood
of choice (cherry
shown here)

Two-Slat Ladderback Chair

This is an occasional chair which lacks the comfort of the four-slat but can be stored easily. The Shakers often hung these from pegs when they were not in use. The dimensions of this chair are identical to the others except for the height of the back legs, therefore the same dowel sizes can be used.

MATERIALS: 3 1 1/4" x 36" maple dowels
6 3/4" x 36" dowels
1 1/4" x 6" x 20" hardwood

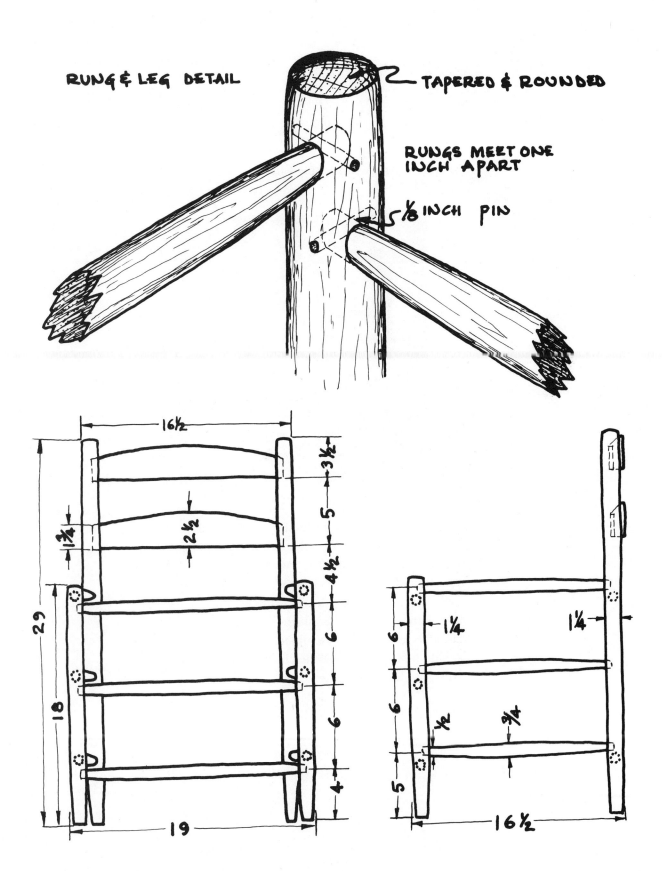

RUNG & LEG DETAIL

TAPERED & ROUNDED

RUNGS MEET ONE INCH APART

⅝ INCH PIN

16½

3½

5

2½

1¾

4½

29

6

18

6

19

4

6

6

1¼

1¼

½

¾

5

16½

Armless Rocking Chair

The armless rocker was popular with Shakers, and many can be found in museum collections today. A hundred and fifty years ago this rocker, called a slipper chair, was used in the bedroom for dressing. To guarantee a good alignment, slots for the ash rockers should be cut after the chair is assembled. The rockers should be fitted so that the chair sets fairly straight when not in use.

MATERIALS: 3 48" x 1¼" hardwood dowels
6 36" x ¾" dowels
1 board foot hardwood
2 board feet white ash

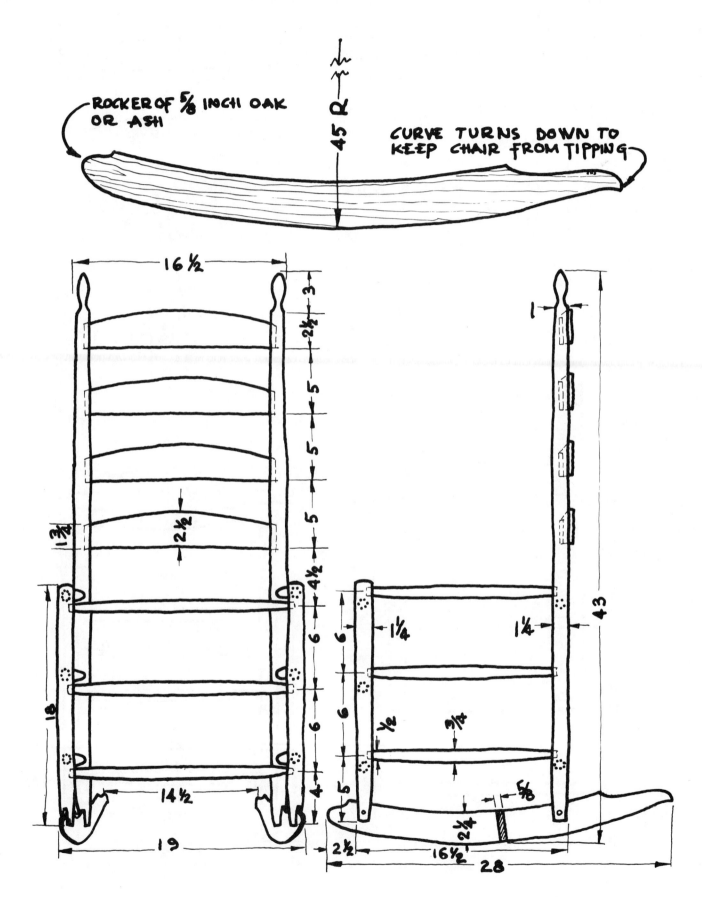

ROCKER OF ⅝ INCH OAK OR ASH

CURVE TURNS DOWN TO KEEP CHAIR FROM TIPPING

45 R

16½

3

2½

5

5

5

4½

2½

1¾

6

6

18

14½

19

4

1

43

1¼

1¼

6

6

6

½

¾

5

2½

16½

2¼

⅝

28

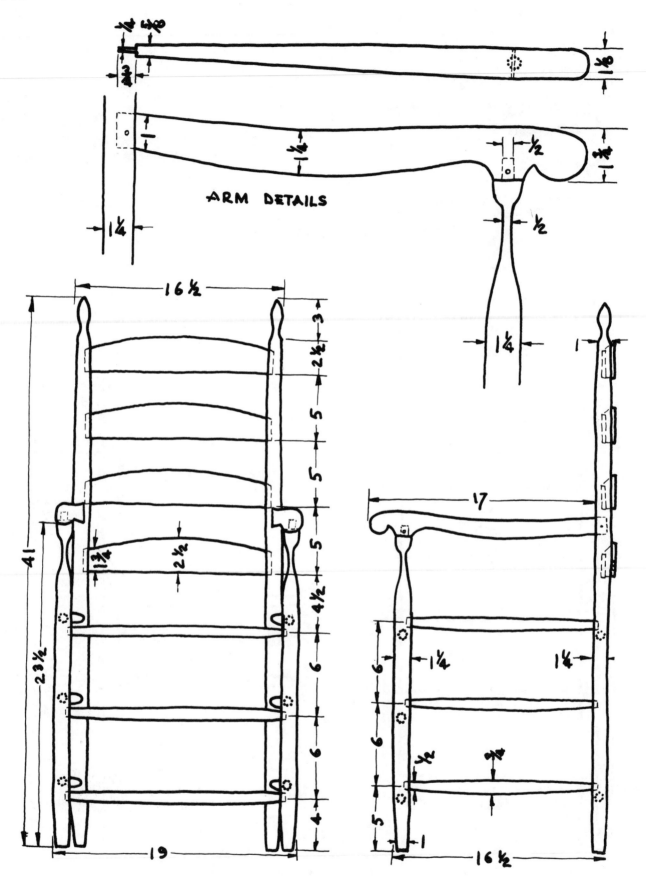

ARM DETAILS

Armchair

This is simply a four-slat ladderback
chair with longer front legs and arms.
Attach the arms after the chair is fully
assembled and pin them securely.

MATERIALS: 4 48" x 1¼" dowels
6 36" x ¾" dowels
3 board feet hardwood

Low Foot Stool

Using mostly scraps from chair construction, this stool is easily made. The top rungs need not be pinned since the tension in the seat will hold things together.

MATERIALS: 1 48" x 1 1/4" dowel
2 36" x 3/4" dowels

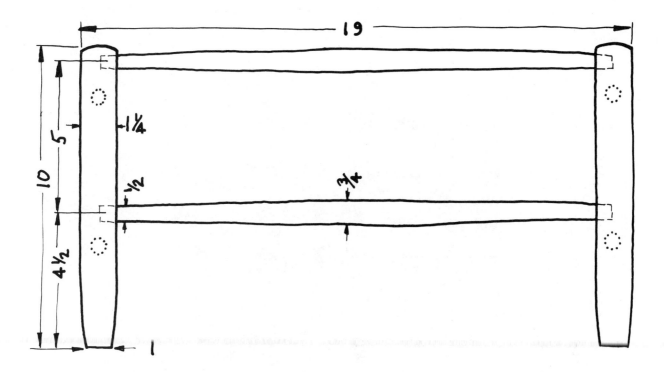

19

10

5

4½

1¼

½

¾

1

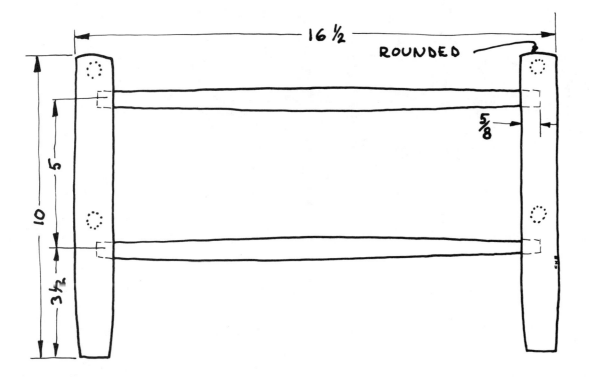

16½

ROUNDED

10

5

3½

⅝

Built to go with the standing desk, this stool uses the same construction techniques as the chairs already described. If the high stool is to go in a special place, allow seven or eight inches between the top of the stool seat and the bottom of the desk or table apron to allow room for a person's legs.

MATERIALS: 8 lengths ¾" x 36" dowel
 4 1¼" x 42" maple dowels
 1 ¼" x 6" x 20" hardwood

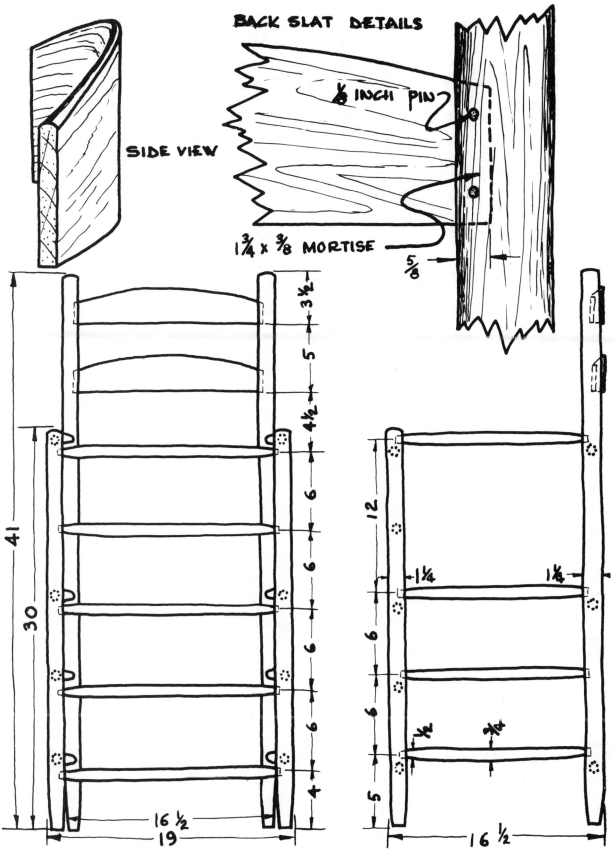

BACK SLAT DETAILS

SIDE VIEW

⅛ INCH PIN

1¾ x ⅜ MORTISE

⅝

3½

5

4½

6

6

6

6

4

41

30

16½
19

12

1¼   1¼

6

6

½   ¾

5

16½

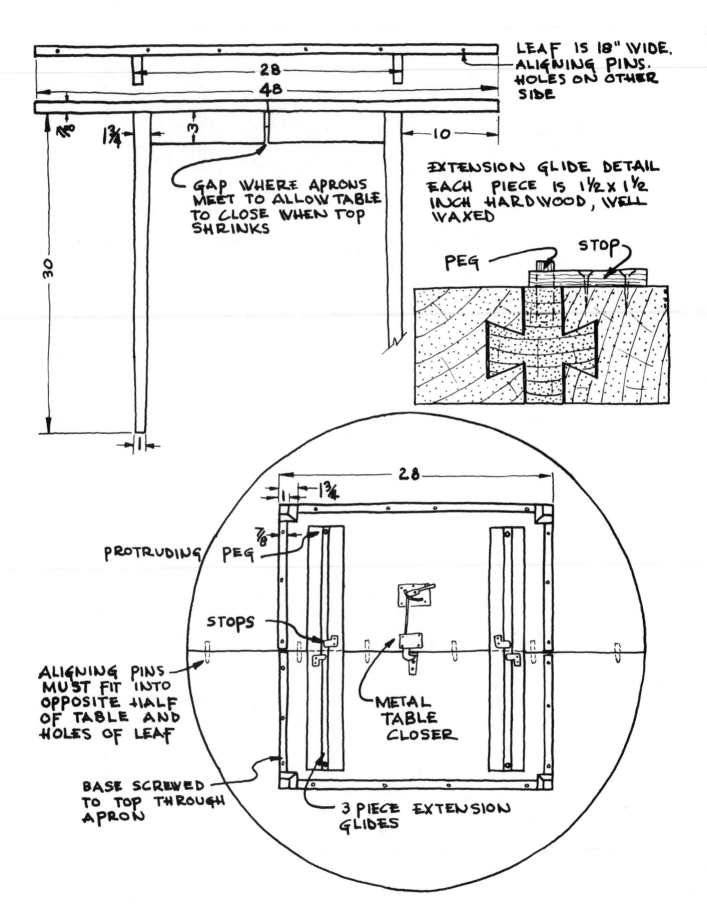

LEAF IS 18" WIDE.
ALIGNING PINS.
HOLES ON OTHER
SIDE

28
48

1¾
3
10

30

1

GAP WHERE APRONS
MEET TO ALLOW TABLE
TO CLOSE WHEN TOP
SHRINKS

EXTENSION GLIDE DETAIL
EACH PIECE IS 1½ X 1½
INCH HARDWOOD, WELL
WAXED

PEG
STOP

28
1
1¾
⅞

PROTRUDING PEG

STOPS

ALIGNING PINS
MUST FIT INTO
OPPOSITE HALF
OF TABLE AND
HOLES OF LEAF

METAL
TABLE
CLOSER

BASE SCREWED
TO TOP THROUGH
APRON

3 PIECE EXTENSION
GLIDES

Round Extension Table

The Shakers did not build an extension table, so far as I know. They didn't live in apartments as many of us do today, and they usually dined at much larger, permanently situated tables. This table is ideal for four people, and six can squeeze in without the leaf. With the eighteen-inch leaf in place the table opens to five and a half feet overall and is perfect for six, but it can accommodate seven or eight in a pinch. The only difficult part in this design is the extension glide, which must be built so that it slides open and closed without undue friction. Paraffin wax or, better, silicone spray will facilitate a free movement.

MATERIALS: 32 board feet primary wood
4 board feet hardwood extension material
1 adjustable table leaf lock

Harvest Table

Of all dropleaf designs this one is clearly the most serviceable, for it is designed to take side chairs under the table with the leaves down. This makes it possible to store the table and eight chairs within a space measuring 28 by 88 inches — perfect where space is at a premium. The design is one of simplicity and grace, and can be made from four to eight feet long. Remember, however, that for a table setting you should allow twenty-four inches.

MATERIALS: 38 board feet primary wood
6 1 1/2" table leaf hinges

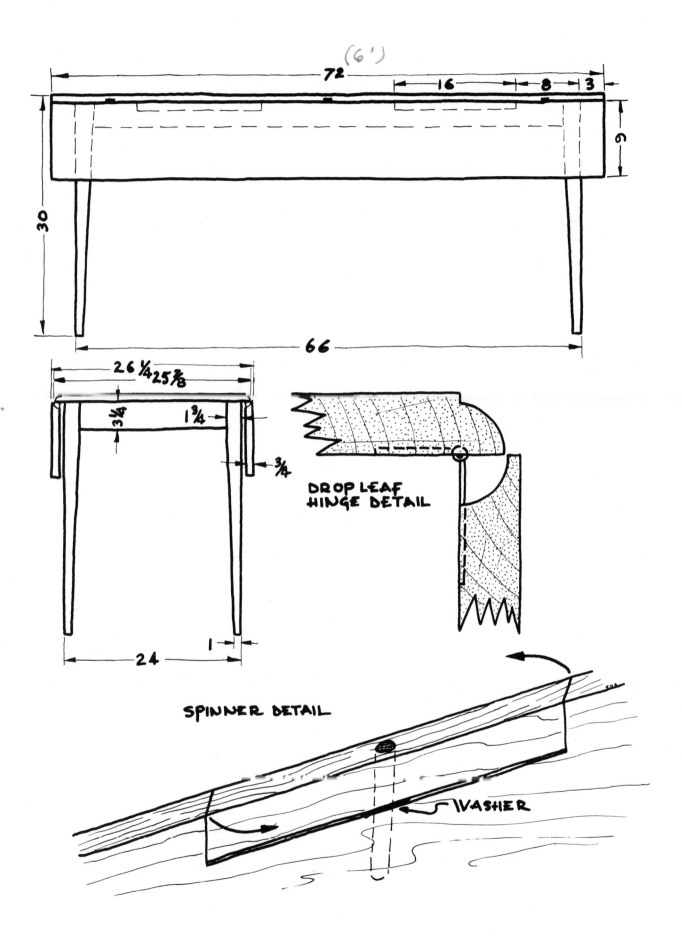

(6')

72

16

8

3

9

30

66

26 1/4

25 7/8

3 3/4

1 3/4

3/4

24

1

DROP LEAF
HINGE DETAIL

SPINNER DETAIL

WASHER

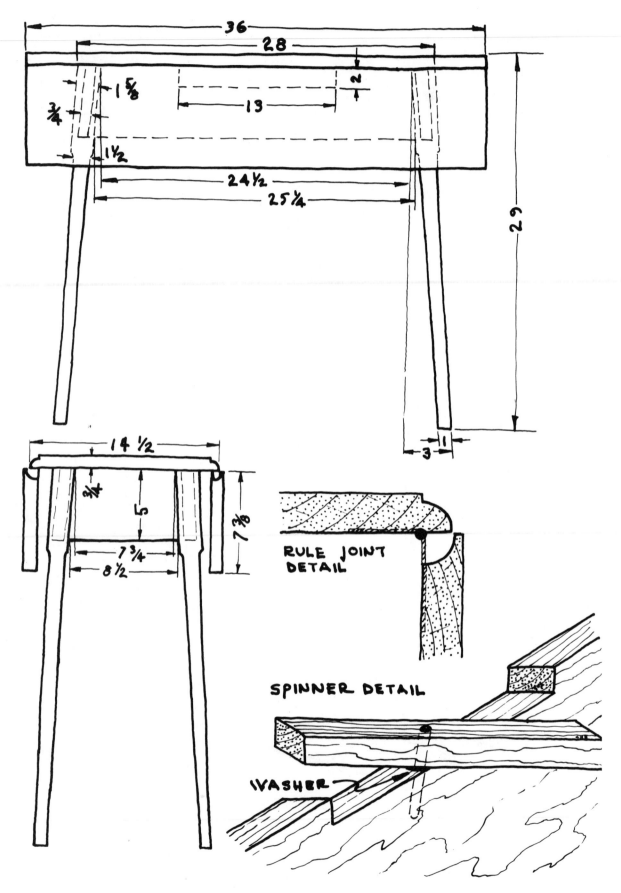

RULE JOINT
DETAIL

SPINNER DETAIL

WASHER

Splay-Leg Dropleaf Table

As an occasional table which can also be used to seat four (in something less than luxury), this table is ideal. The splay is achieved by cutting tenon shoulders at a slight angle. This same angle must be repeated in cutting the leaf-support spinner slot so that the support swings out in a horizontal position. The spinner, too, is pinned at a slight angle.

MATERIALS: 18 board feet primary wood
4 1½" steel table hinges

Stretcher Table

The double urn and rings on the legs may place this table outside of Shaker form. Also called a tavern table, this design offers stability and pleasant proportions. As a desk it is ideal. Most tables of this sort had four stretchers running from leg to leg. Although this adds strength, it precludes passing a chair beneath the table on all four sides. By replacing the two side stretchers with a single center stretcher, side chairs can be accommodated.

MATERIALS: 33 board feet primary wood
            5 board feet secondary wood

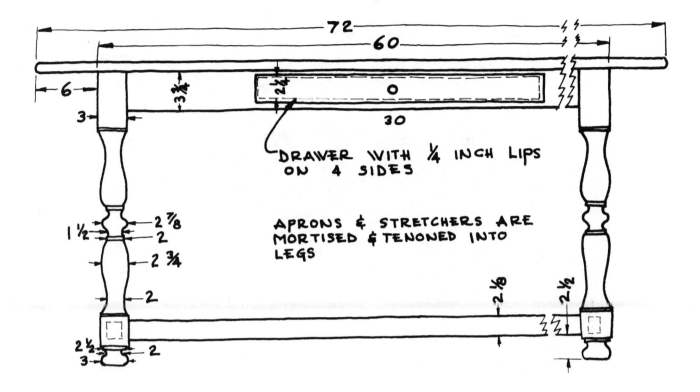

72

60

6

3 3/4

2 1/4   o

30

DRAWER WITH 1/4 INCH LIPS
ON 4 SIDES

APRONS & STRETCHERS ARE
MORTISED & TENONED INTO
LEGS

1 1/2   2 7/8
2
2 3/4

2

2 1/2   2
3

2 1/8   2 1/2

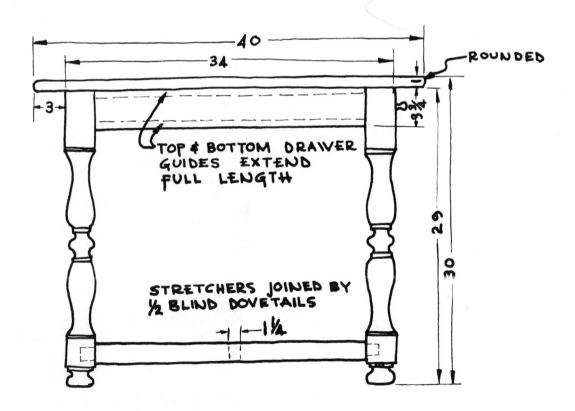

40

34

ROUNDED

3

3 3/4

TOP & BOTTOM DRAWER
GUIDES EXTEND
FULL LENGTH

29

30

STRETCHERS JOINED BY
1/2 BLIND DOVETAILS

1 1/2

Chair Table

Chair tables were a popular form in
the nineteenth century, and it appears
that the Shakers not only were famil-
iar with them but also built them for
their own use. The great advantage of
this style is the ability to store it when
not in use. With the top tilted up, the
base becomes a functional, if uncom-
fortable, chair with drawer included

MATERIALS:
50 board feet primary wood
9 board feet secondary wood
Polished brass hinges and lock

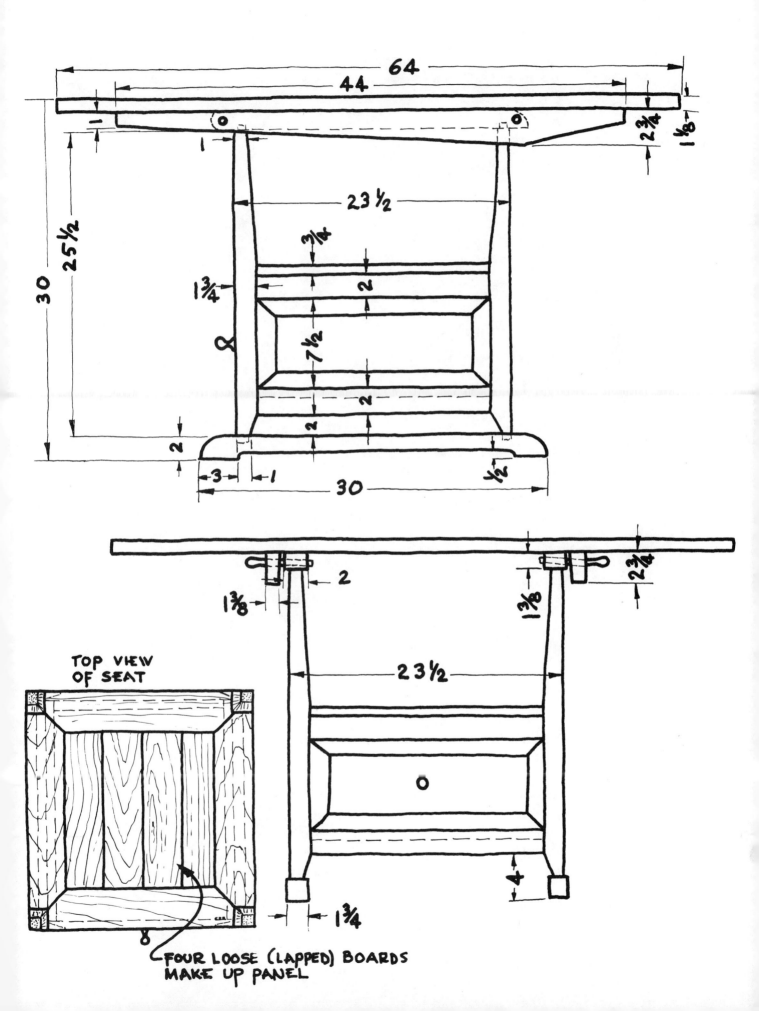

TOP VIEW OF SEAT

FOUR LOOSE (LAPPED) BOARDS MAKE UP PANEL

Five-Drawer Chest

Having experimented with a number of sizes and proportions, we feel that this chest of drawers represents an ideal form. The lower drawer can take bulky sweaters, even a coat in storage, while the top drawers are not so deep as to lose small items in dark recesses. Notice that the chest is designed without an applied face, which greatly simplifies construction. Remember, do not firmly glue drawer dividers or mouldings to sides; rather, use brads to avoid checking in winter. The plain lines of this piece accentuate the activity of the top dovetails, which make a delightful visual discovery.

MATERIALS: 36 board feet primary wood
30 board feet secondary wood

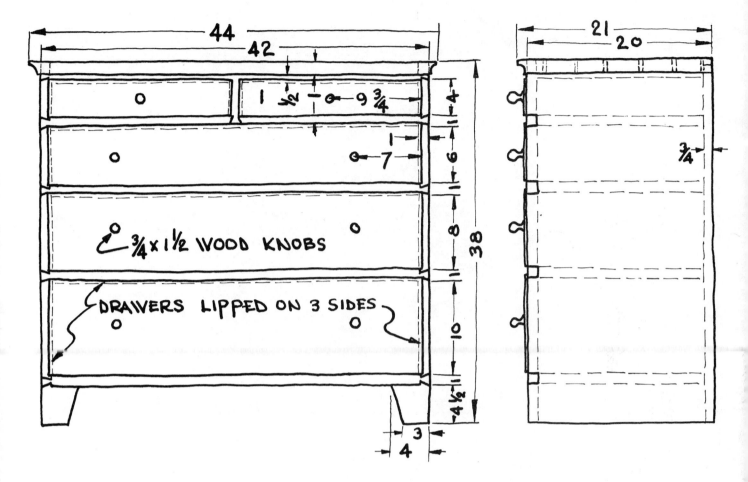

44
42

1 ½ — 9 ¾

1
7

¾ x 1½ WOOD KNOBS

DRAWERS LIPPED ON 3 SIDES

4
1
6
8
10
4½
38

3
4

21
20

¾

TOP MOULDING

¼
1
¼
1

SIDES ARE DOVETAILED THROUGH TOP

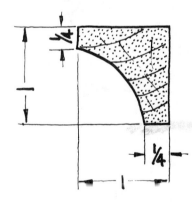

Ten-Drawer Chest

Most people who see the ten-drawer chest for the first time think it's made for a basketball player. It isn't really. With a step stool the average adult can get to the top of things while the child will view the top drawers as totally inaccessible. And this is one reason for its design — the top drawers are private spaces. If you like cutting dovetails, you'll love building this chest with its two hundred or so dovetails.

MATERIALS: 70 board feet primary wood
76 board feet secondary wood

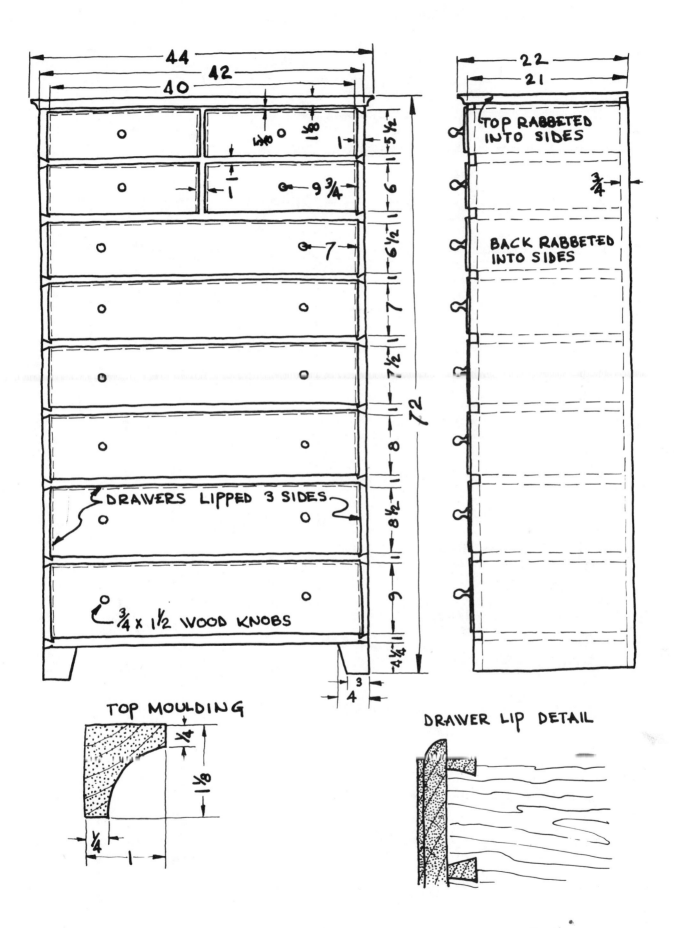

44
42
40
5½
6
9¾
6½
7
7½
72
8
8½
9
4¾
3
4

22
21
¾

TOP RABBETED INTO SIDES

BACK RABBETED INTO SIDES

7

DRAWERS LIPPED 3 SIDES

¾ x 1½ WOOD KNOBS

TOP MOULDING

¼
1⅛
¼
1

DRAWER LIP DETAIL

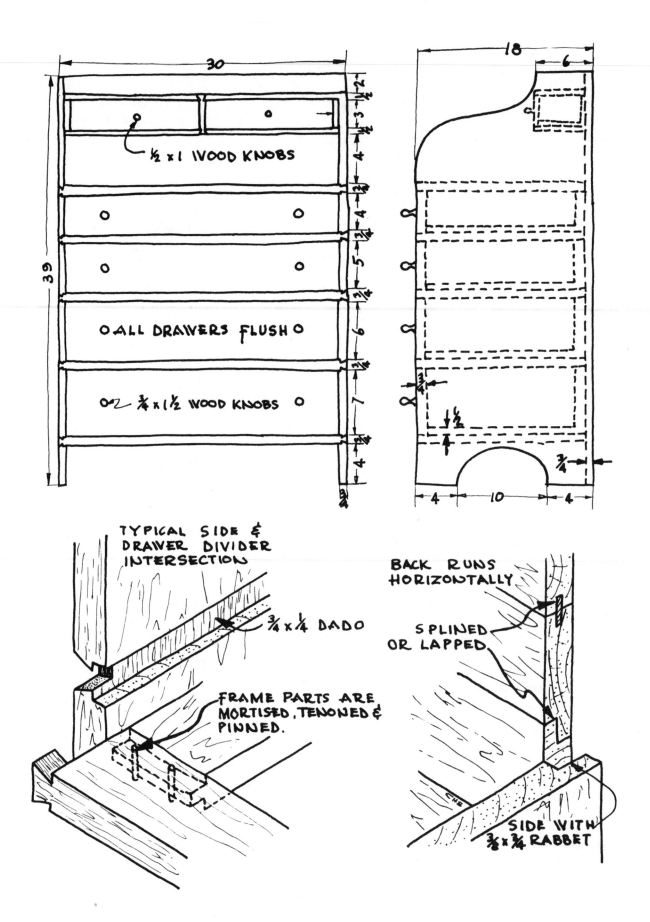

½ x 1 WOOD KNOBS

O ALL DRAWERS FLUSH O

O ¾ x 1½ WOOD KNOBS O

30

39

18

6

TYPICAL SIDE &
DRAWER DIVIDER
INTERSECTION

¾ x ¼ DADO

FRAME PARTS ARE
MORTISED, TENONED &
PINNED.

BACK RUNS
HORIZONTALLY

SPLINED
OR LAPPED

SIDE WITH
⅜ x ¾ RABBET

Sewing Desk

Almost a miniature, the sewing desk offers six small drawers for a wide range of uses. It is actually a chest of flush front drawers with an open work shelf at the top. One very much like it is in the Shaker collection at Sabbathday Lake, Maine.

MATERIALS: 28 board feet primary wood
35 board feet secondary wood

Two-Drawer Blanket Box

The use of rabbeted joints makes this a fairly easy case to build. The drawer construction is the same as in the other case pieces and should present no obstacle. Notice that the grain direction of the front and back boards runs at right angles to the grain direction in the side boards. This will result in dimensional change as great as 3/16 inch from winter to summer. Do not glue these joints. Use either finish nails, old-fashioned rosehead nails, or screws.

MATERIALS: 34 board feet primary wood
32 board feet secondary wood

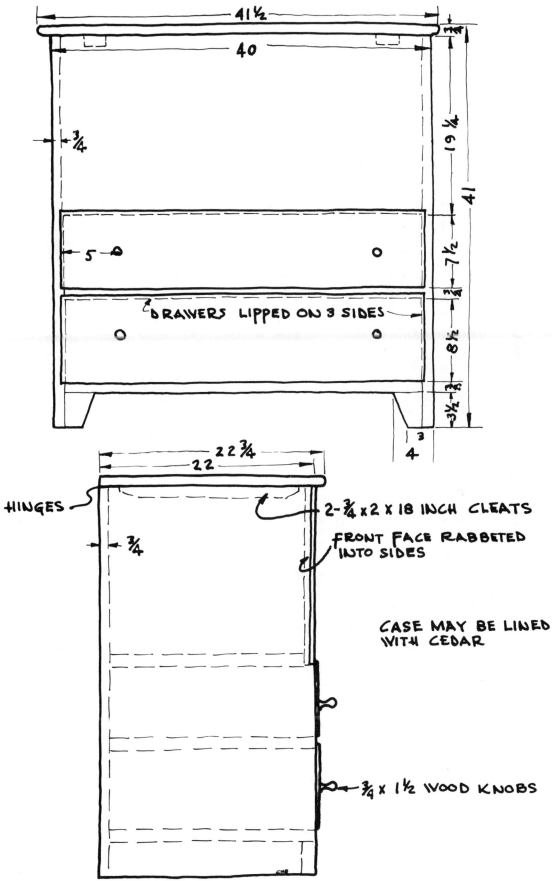

41½

40

¾

19¼

41

5

7½

¾

DRAWERS LIPPED ON 3 SIDES

8½

3½

3

3

4

22¾

22

HINGES

¾

2-¾ x 2 x 18 INCH CLEATS

FRONT FACE RABBETED INTO SIDES

CASE MAY BE LINED WITH CEDAR

¾ x 1½ WOOD KNOBS

Settee

What distinguishes this bench from the Shaker settee of the nineteenth
century is the use of the arched leg supports. The inspiration for the
supports is the ship's knee, a diagonal support made from a naturally bent
tree member (usually where a limb grows out of the trunk). Made of hack-
matack or oak, ship's knees gave considerable support to crucial joints.
Our "knee" derives its strength from wood lamination. Five pieces glued
under pressure in a form provide unbelievable strength. Two forms, a
male and female, are cut in the shape of an arch and five 1/8 inch x 3/4 inch
x 24 inch strips are glued together using five or six clamps for pressure. Once
set up, this becomes almost unbreakable. Notice, too, that the legs are
fastened to the seat with glue and wedged similarly to an ax handle. Use
maple in the legs and hickory or ash in the back spindles.

MATERIALS: 21 board feet primary wood
             4 board feet rock maple
             30 lineal feet 1/2" square ash stock

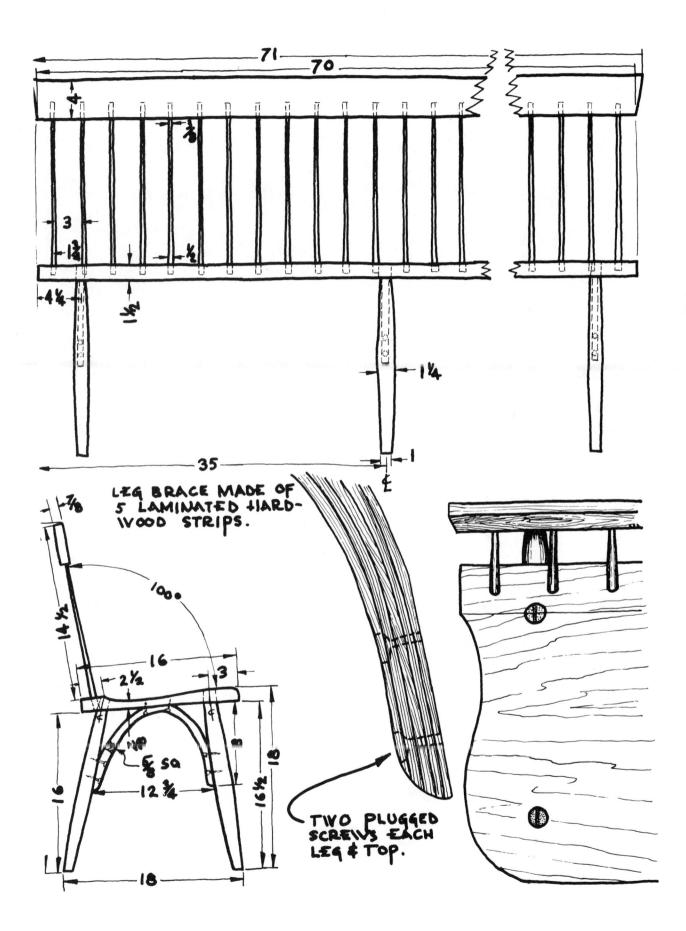

LEG BRACE MADE OF
5 LAMINATED HARD-
WOOD STRIPS.

TWO PLUGGED
SCREWS EACH
LEG & TOP.

Low-Post Bed

This design can be used for queen-, full-, and twin-size mattresses and box springs. Mattresses and springs come in standard sizes (twin, 39" x 74"; full, 54" x 74"; queen, 60" x 80"), but since they vary according to manufacturer, they should be measured before cutting the rails. The footboard and headboard are permanently joined with pegged mortise and tenons while the side rails are removable. The bed can be taken down by simply removing the four bed bolts. The mattress hangers are cut from 1/4 inch x 4 inch angle iron and should be attached to the inside of the side rails in order to hold the box springs. Since most modern mattresses and box springs combine to 14-inch height overall, the hangers are placed at the very lowest edge of the rail. If your mattress and spring are shallow, then obviously the hanger should be raised accordingly.

MATERIALS: 28 board feet primary wood
4 7-inch bed bolts
6 1/4" x 4" x 2" angle irons

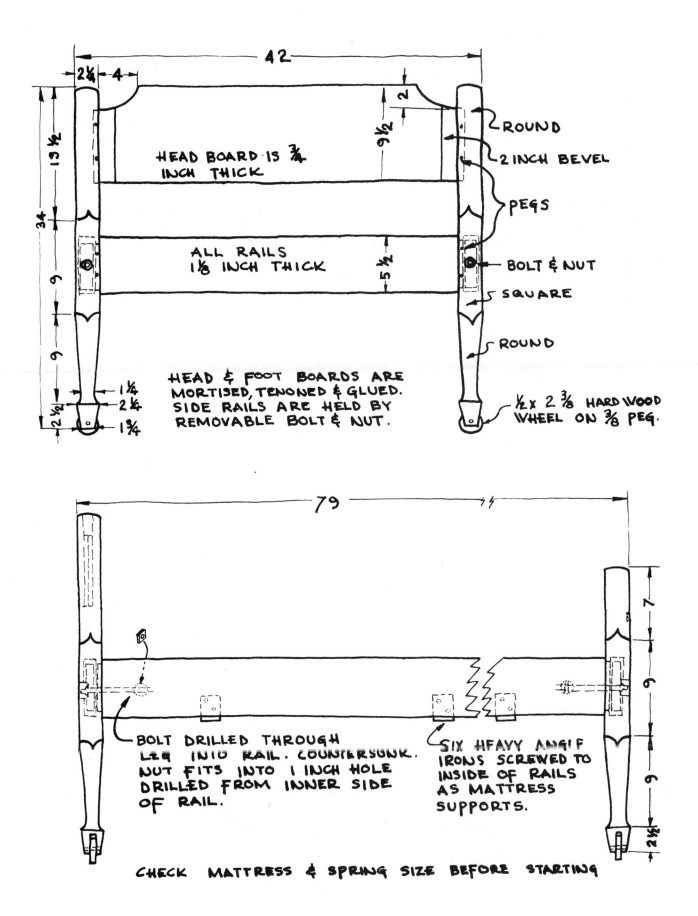

42

2¼ 4

13½

34

9

9

1¼
2¼
2½
1¾

HEAD BOARD IS ¾ INCH THICK

ALL RAILS 1⅛ INCH THICK

HEAD & FOOT BOARDS ARE MORTISED, TENONED & GLUED. SIDE RAILS ARE HELD BY REMOVABLE BOLT & NUT.

2

9½

5½

ROUND

2 INCH BEVEL

PEGS

BOLT & NUT

SQUARE

ROUND

½ x 2⅜ HARDWOOD WHEEL ON ⅜ PEG.

79

7

6

6

2½

BOLT DRILLED THROUGH LEG INTO RAIL. COUNTERSUNK. NUT FITS INTO 1 INCH HOLE DRILLED FROM INNER SIDE OF RAIL.

SIX HEAVY ANGLE IRONS SCREWED TO INSIDE OF RAILS AS MATTRESS SUPPORTS.

CHECK MATTRESS & SPRING SIZE BEFORE STARTING

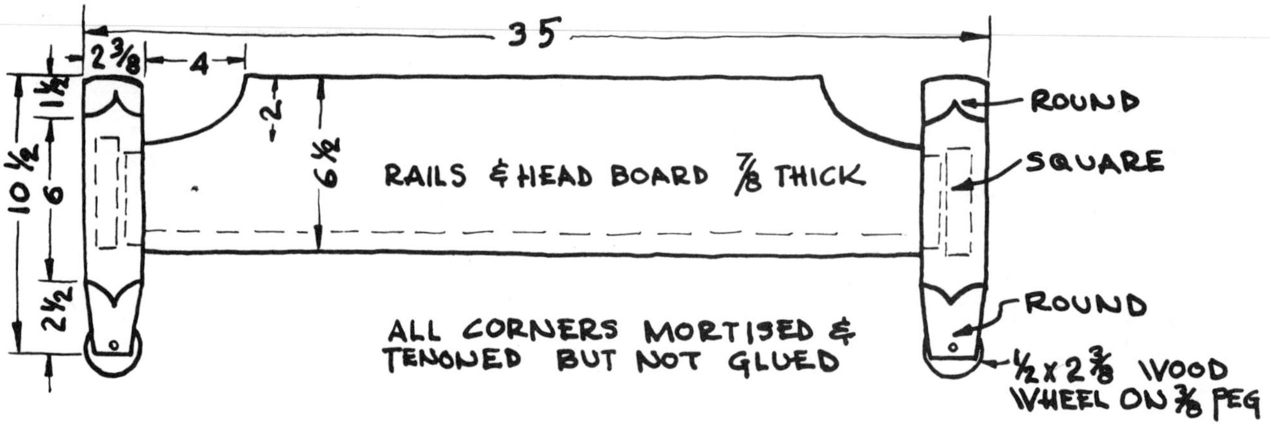
35
2 3/8
4
1 1/2
2
10 1/2
6
6 1/2
2 1/2
RAILS & HEAD BOARD 7/8 THICK
ROUND
SQUARE
ROUND
ALL CORNERS MORTISED & TENONED BUT NOT GLUED
1/2 x 2 3/8 WOOD WHEEL ON 3/8 PEG

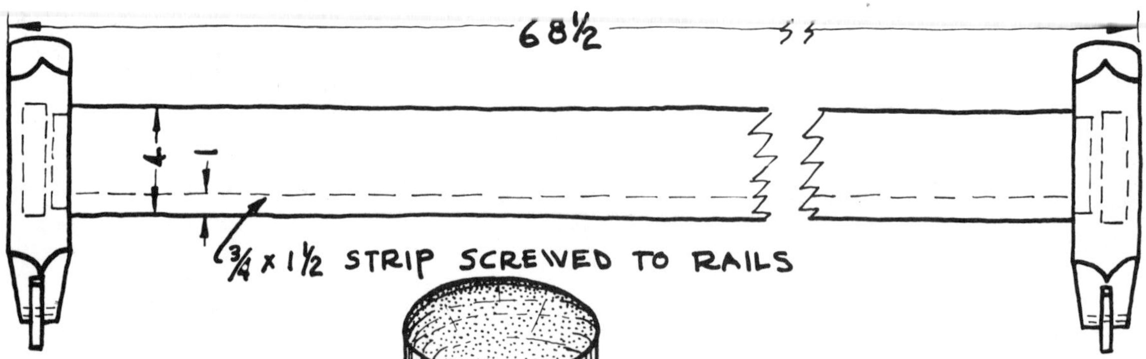
68 1/2
4
1
3/4 x 1 1/2 STRIP SCREWED TO RAILS

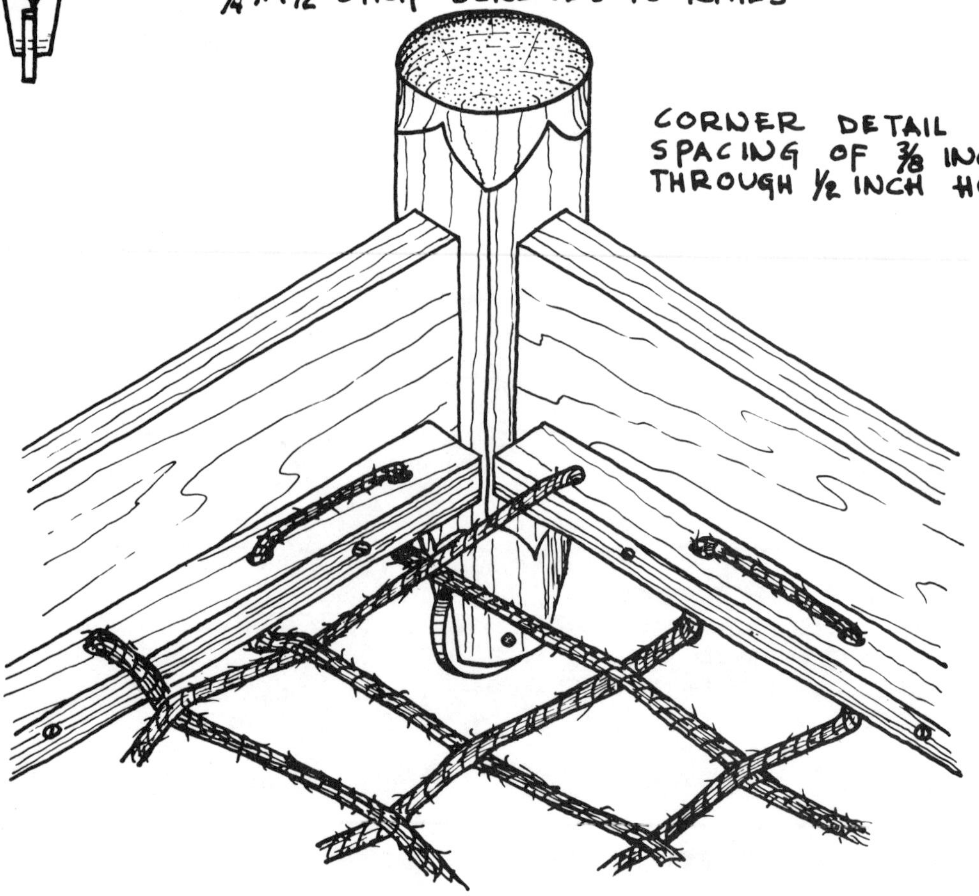

CORNER DETAIL SHOWING SPACING OF 3/8 INCH ROPE THROUGH 1/2 INCH HOLES.

Trundle Bed

In years past, trundle beds were used regularly by small children and were conveniently rolled under the parents' large bed in the morning. I don't know if the Shakers ever used one, but for us today it makes an ideal roll-away for small guests. This one is designed to take a 30-inch mattress, which is a standard cot width. However, since the bed's interior is only 64 inches long, the cot mattress will have to be shortened.

MATERIALS: 12 board feet primary wood
108 feet 3/8" rope

Double Cupboard

According to Edward Andrews there stood in the subcellar of the First Order dwelling, Church Family, New Lebanon, a pine double cupboard which measured 75½ inches high (36 inches from sill to floor and 39½ inches from sill to top) and 19¾ inches wide. Our first attempt was close to this in measurements, but with each new try, proportions changed slightly and two sets of dovetails were added. All of this resulted in the double cupboard pictured here. Joining the top and front shelf to the sides is difficult, but once achieved the rest goes together fairly well.

MATERIALS: 40 board feet primary wood
28 board feet secondary wood

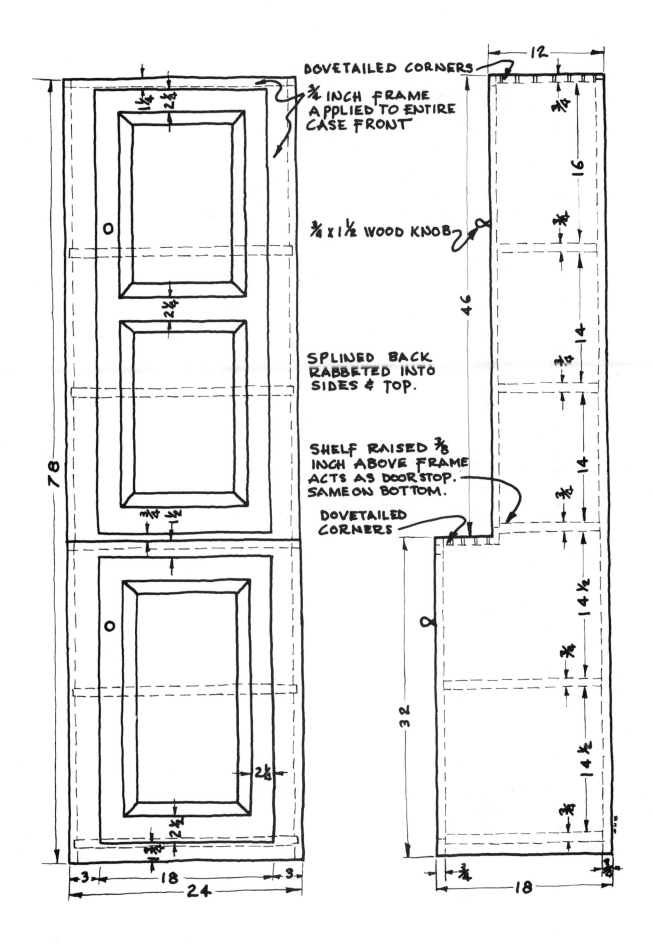

DOVETAILED CORNERS

3/4 INCH FRAME
APPLIED TO ENTIRE
CASE FRONT

3/4 × 1 1/2 WOOD KNOB

SPLINED BACK
RABBETED INTO
SIDES & TOP.

SHELF RAISED 3/8
INCH ABOVE FRAME
ACTS AS DOOR STOP.
SAME ON BOTTOM.

DOVETAILED
CORNERS

Standing Desk

Desks of this kind were usually found in mills, counting houses, or shops where recording transactions were a required part of a day's work. I cannot look at one without thinking of Bob Cratchett and Ebenezer Scrooge. I had a schoolmate who wrote a doctoral dissertation on a desk similar to this. He found that standing up was the only way to stay awake through the long ordeal. The through tenon offers a great opportunity for using decorative wedges. The desk can be made with or without pigeonholes. If used, the top rack can be attached to the base by two small brass cleats screwed to the back. A single brass leaf hinge will work well.

MATERIALS: 33 board feet primary wood
                        12 board feet secondary wood

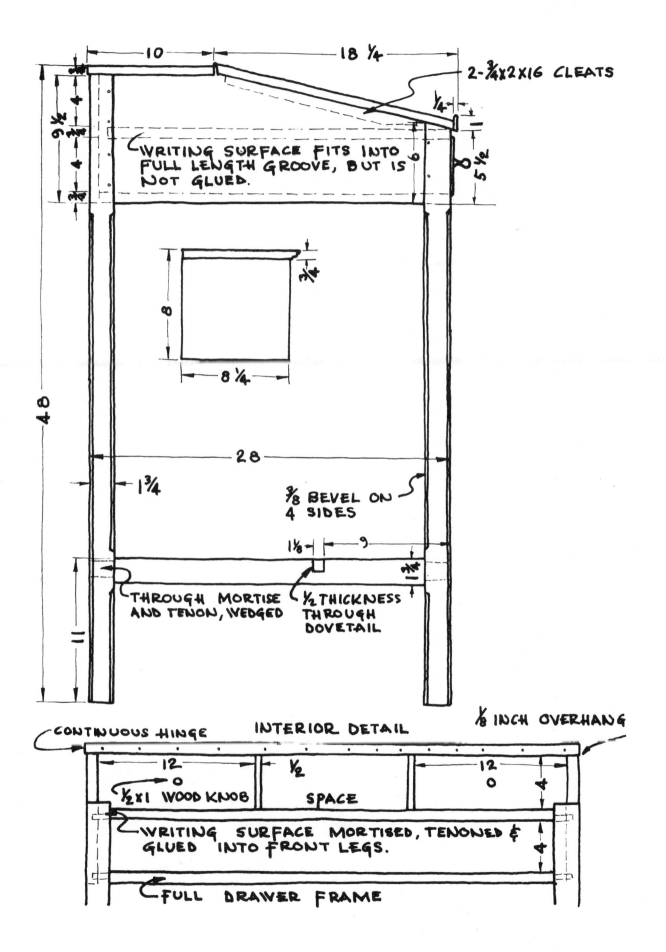

10   18 ¼   2-¾x2x16 CLEATS

48

9/16   ¾   ¼   ¾

¼   5½   6

WRITING SURFACE FITS INTO
FULL LENGTH GROOVE, BUT IS
NOT GLUED.

¾

8   8 ¼

28

1 ¾

⅜ BEVEL ON
4 SIDES

1⅛   9   ¾

THROUGH MORTISE
AND TENON, WEDGED

½ THICKNESS
THROUGH
DOVETAIL

CONTINUOUS HINGE   INTERIOR DETAIL   ⅛ INCH OVERHANG

12   ½   12   4

½x1 WOOD KNOB   SPACE

WRITING SURFACE MORTISED, TENONED &
GLUED INTO FRONT LEGS.

4

FULL DRAWER FRAME

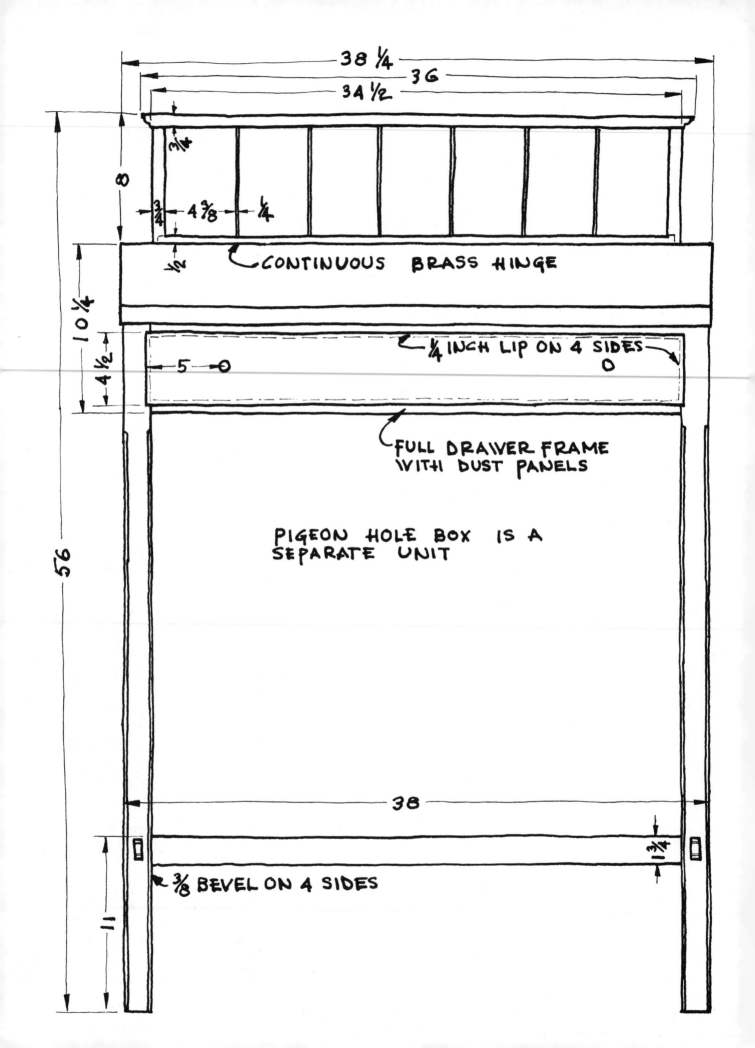

38 ¼

36

34 ½

¾

8

¾   4 ⅜   ¼

½   CONTINUOUS BRASS HINGE

10 ¼

4 ½

¼ INCH LIP ON 4 SIDES

5   O

O

FULL DRAWER FRAME
WITH DUST PANELS

PIGEON HOLE BOX IS A
SEPARATE UNIT

56

38

1 ¾

⅜ BEVEL ON 4 SIDES

11

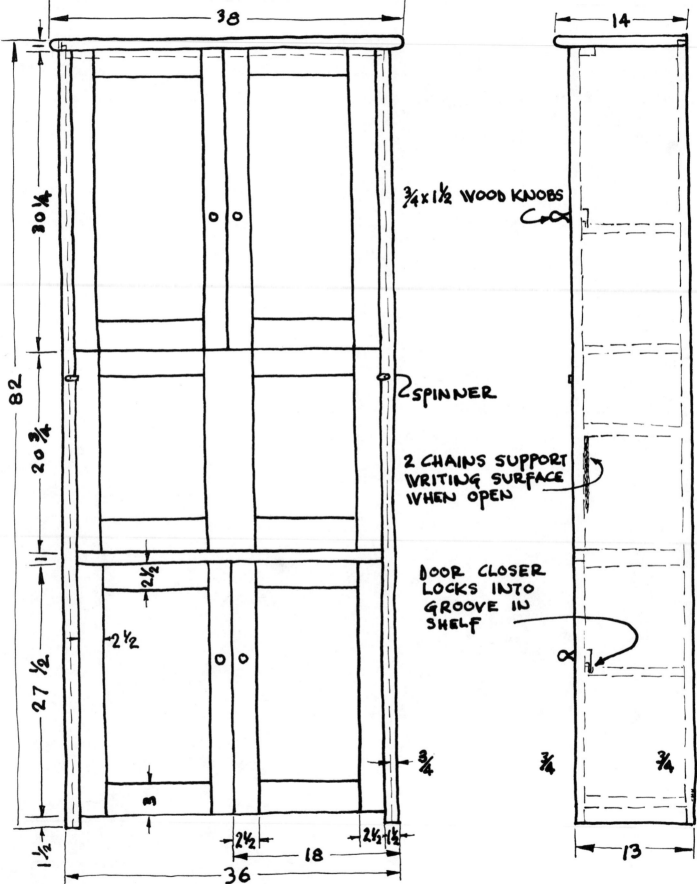

3/4 x 1 1/2 WOOD KNOBS

SPINNER

2 CHAINS SUPPORT WRITING SURFACE WHEN OPEN

DOOR CLOSER LOCKS INTO GROOVE IN SHELF

Kitchen Desk

An enormous undertaking is the building of the kitchen desk. This piece is designed to be used against a wall where it can be anchored with screw or toggle bolt. While the case itself is quite simple, the doors, especially the center writing surface, require extreme care in mounting if an even fit is to be achieved. The chain supports are attached after the door is permanently in place.

MATERIALS:
70 board feet primary wood
24 board feet secondary wood

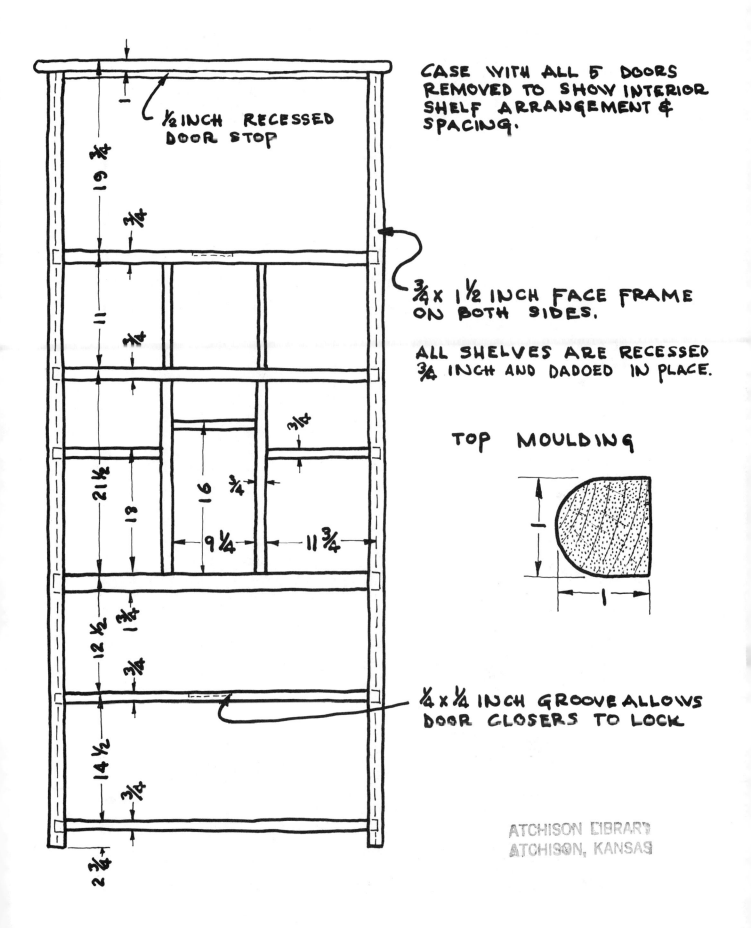

CASE WITH ALL 5 DOORS
REMOVED TO SHOW INTERIOR
SHELF ARRANGEMENT &
SPACING.

½ INCH RECESSED
DOOR STOP

¾ x 1½ INCH FACE FRAME
ON BOTH SIDES.

ALL SHELVES ARE RECESSED
¾ INCH AND DADOED IN PLACE.

TOP MOULDING

¼ x ¼ INCH GROOVE ALLOWS
DOOR CLOSERS TO LOCK

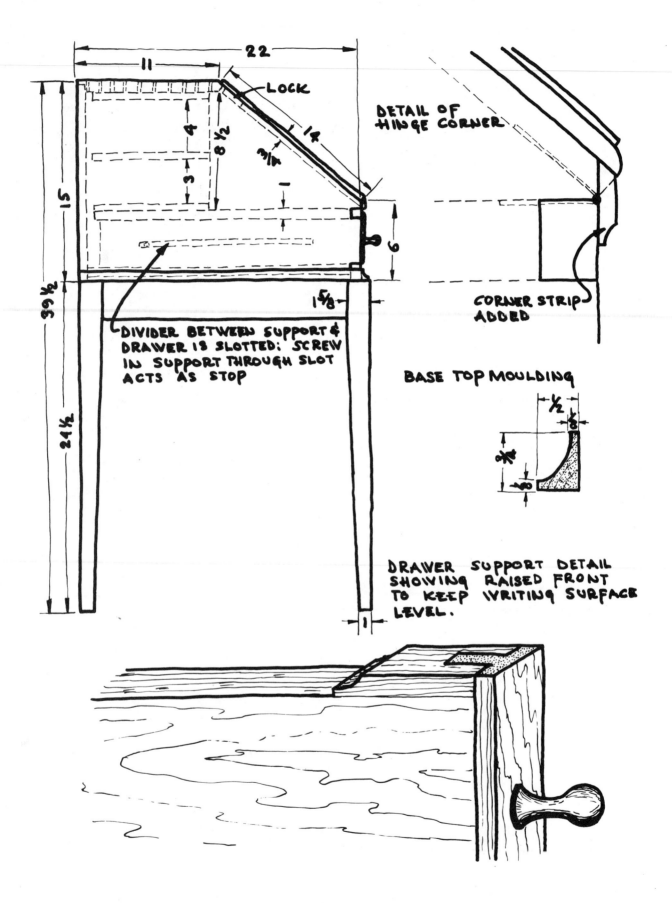

22

11

LOCK

14

3/4

4

8½

3

51

39½

24½

1⅝

6

DETAIL OF HINGE CORNER

CORNER STRIP ADDED

DIVIDER BETWEEN SUPPORT & DRAWER IS SLOTTED; SCREW IN SUPPORT THROUGH SLOT ACTS AS STOP

BASE TOP MOULDING

½

DRAWER SUPPORT DETAIL SHOWING RAISED FRONT TO KEEP WRITING SURFACE LEVEL.

1

Small Writing Desk

This design incorporates the best elements of a slant-top desk with the best elements of a writing table. It is altogether practical and pleasing to the eye. The most difficult aspect is building and installing the hinged writing surface. Care must be taken in breadboarding and leveling, since any warp will result in a less than even fit on the case. Although intricate in detail, this piece when finished is well worth the effort.

MATERIALS: 50 board feet primary wood
9 board feet secondary wood
Polished brass hinges and lock

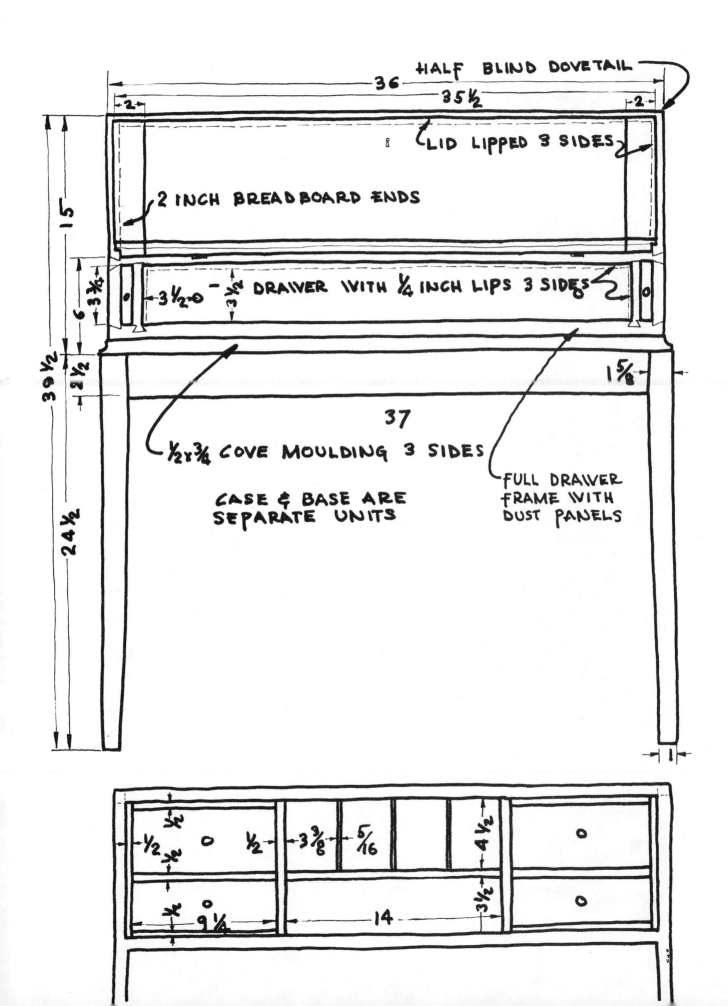

HALF BLIND DOVETAIL

36

35½

2   2

LID LIPPED 3 SIDES

8

15

2 INCH BREADBOARD ENDS

3⅜

6   0   3½-0   3" DRAIVER WITH ¼ INCH LIPS 3 SIDES   0

39½

2½

1⅝

37

½×¾ COVE MOULDING 3 SIDES

CASE & BASE ARE
SEPARATE UNITS

FULL DRAIVER
FRAME WITH
DUST PANELS

24½

1

½

½ ½   0   ½   3⅜   5/16   4½

3½

0

½   0   9½   14   3½   0

Tall Clock

The term "tall clock" was used throughout the eighteenth and early nineteenth centuries to describe this class of standing clocks. It was not until a song of 1850 or so, titled "My Grandfather's Clock," became popular that the clock was renamed. To the Shakers, and particularly to Brother Benjamin Youngs, the tall case clock was an excellent form, in that it provided adequate room for a heavy weight to drop a sufficient distance to drive the clock a full week. Most Shaker tall clocks were extremely clean in design, having absolutely no ornament. This clock design is based on one pictured in an Edward and Faith Andrews photograph shown in their book *Shaker Furniture* (1937). It is built in pine and painted a dark red. It has an eight-day weight-driven silent movement. Although pictured with serpentine hands, simple Terry hands or banjo hands are preferred.

MATERIALS: *25 board feet primary wood*
10 board feet secondary wood
9-inch paper dial
8-day, weight-driven, 29-inch pendulum, silent
   movement with plain hands

Model U 17P-74
Crafts Products Company
Elmhurst, Illinois 60126

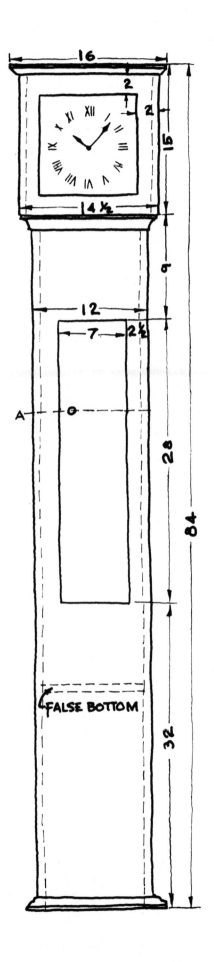
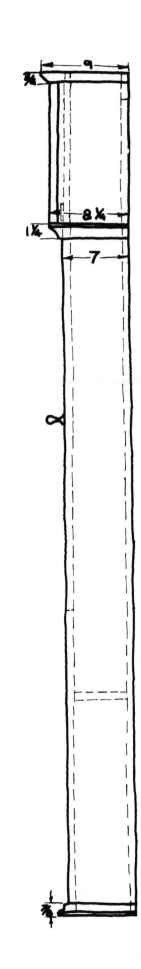

16

2

2

15

14½

9

12

7   2½

A —— O

28

84

FALSE BOTTOM

32

9

¾

8¼

1¼

7

8

¾

MOULDING DETAILS

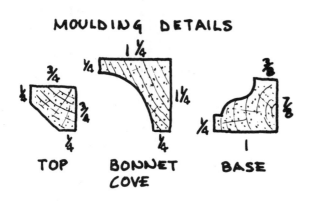

3/4
1/4
3/4
1/4

TOP

1 1/4
1/4
1 1/4
1/4

BONNET
COVE

3/8
7/8
1/4
1

BASE

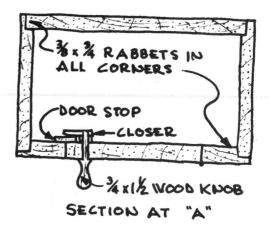

3/8 x 3/4 RABBETS IN ALL CORNERS

DOOR STOP

CLOSER

3/4 x 1 1/2 WOOD KNOB

SECTION AT "A"

BONNET SIDE & BACK BRACE

1/4 x 1 STRIP MORTISED INTO BOTH SIDES OF BONNET

FACE GLUED TO STABLE BOARD & SCREWED TO CLOCK SIDES. MECHANISM MOUNTED ON BACK OF FACE.

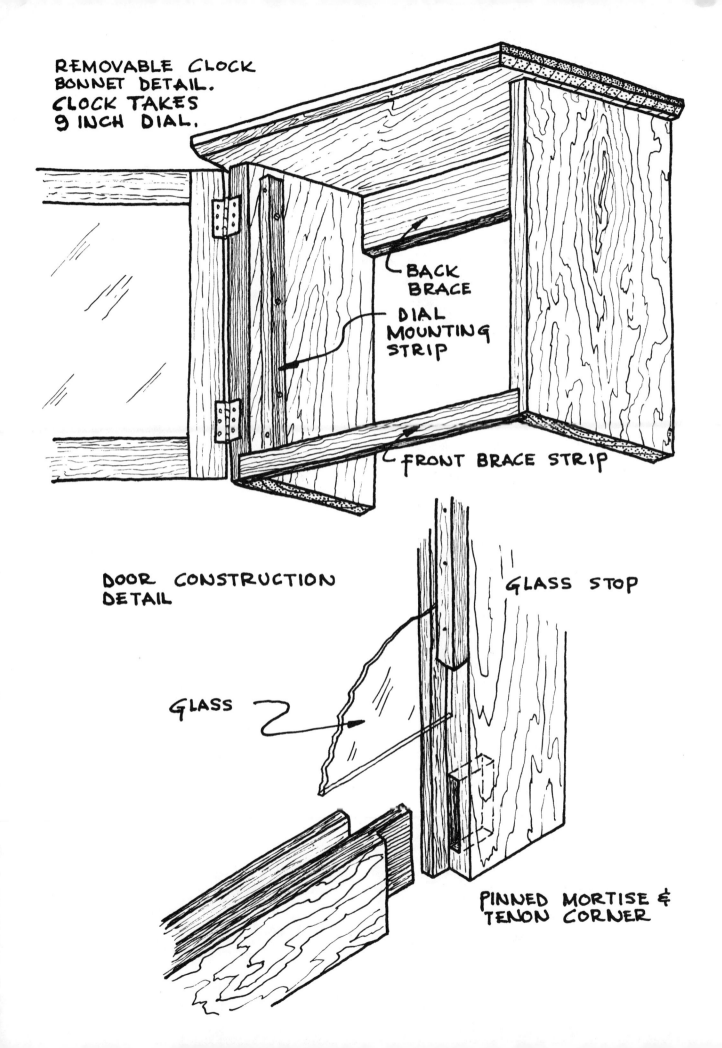

REMOVABLE CLOCK
BONNET DETAIL.
CLOCK TAKES
9 INCH DIAL.

BACK
BRACE

DIAL
MOUNTING
STRIP

FRONT BRACE STRIP

DOOR CONSTRUCTION
DETAIL

GLASS STOP

GLASS

PINNED MORTISE &
TENON CORNER

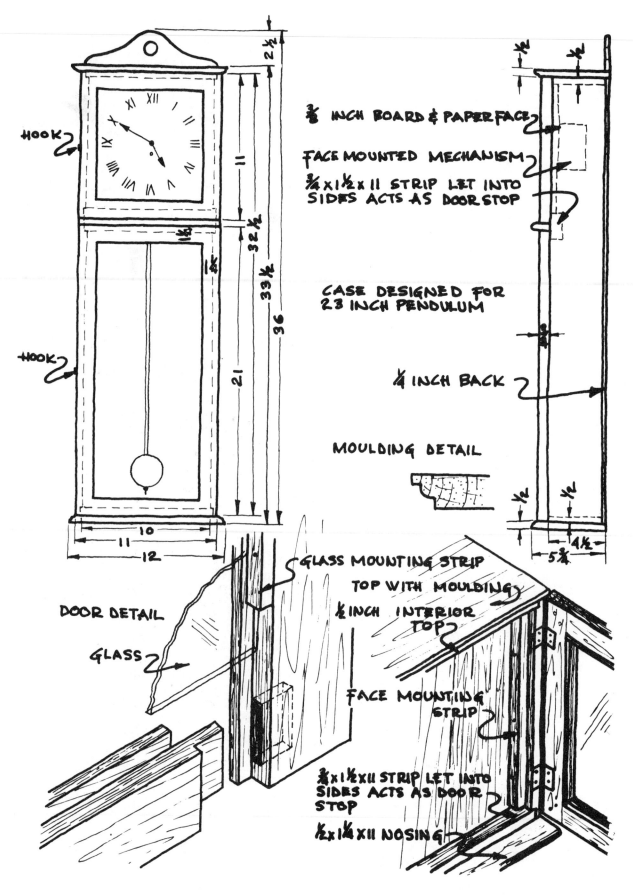

HOOK

HOOK

2½

11

32½

33½

36

21

10

11

12

⅜ INCH BOARD & PAPER FACE

FACE MOUNTED MECHANISM

¾ x 1½ x 11 STRIP LET INTO SIDES ACTS AS DOOR STOP

CASE DESIGNED FOR 23 INCH PENDULUM

¼ INCH BACK

MOULDING DETAIL

½

4½

5¾

DOOR DETAIL

GLASS

GLASS MOUNTING STRIP

TOP WITH MOULDING

½ INCH INTERIOR TOP

FACE MOUNTING STRIP

¾ x 1½ x 11 STRIP LET INTO SIDES ACTS AS DOOR STOP

½ x 1¼ x 11 NOSING

Wall Clock

Being a time-conscious people, the Shakers had a
keen interest in clocks of all sorts, though personal
watches were frowned upon. Among the most
inventive clockmakers were Benjamin and Isaac
Youngs, and their clocks are true collector's items
today. This wall clock is designed from a prototype
built by Isaac Youngs and used in the Hancock
Community in New Hampshire. Like the tall clock
the dial is made of 3/8-inch plywood covered in a
good quality coated paper upon which the numerals
have been drawn in India ink.

MATERIALS: 7 board feet primary wood
2 small brass hooks
1 7-inch paper dial
1 eight-day, spring driven,
pendulum movement

Model U18D W/36
Crafts Products Company
Elmhurst, Illinois 60126

Bathroom Cupboard Adaptation

The prebuilt vanity in most modern bathrooms leaves much to be desired. Pictured here is a seven-foot double sink that was built in black walnut. The top is made of ¾-inch plywood and is covered in an eggshell white plastic laminate. Following the same techniques described throughout this book, one can design a functional, yet appealing bathroom cupboard.

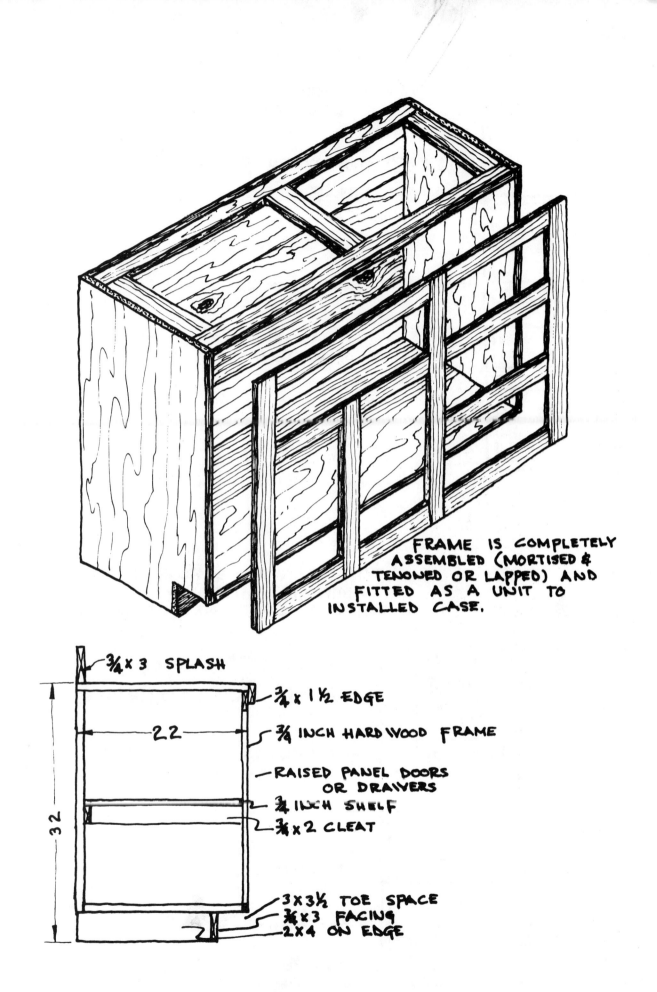

FRAME IS COMPLETELY
ASSEMBLED (MORTISED &
TENONED OR LAPPED) AND
FITTED AS A UNIT TO
INSTALLED CASE.

¾ X 3 SPLASH

¾ X 1½ EDGE

¾ INCH HARDWOOD FRAME

22

RAISED PANEL DOORS
OR DRAWERS

¾ INCH SHELF

¾ X 2 CLEAT

32

3 X 3½ TOE SPACE

¾ X 3 FACING

2 X 4 ON EDGE

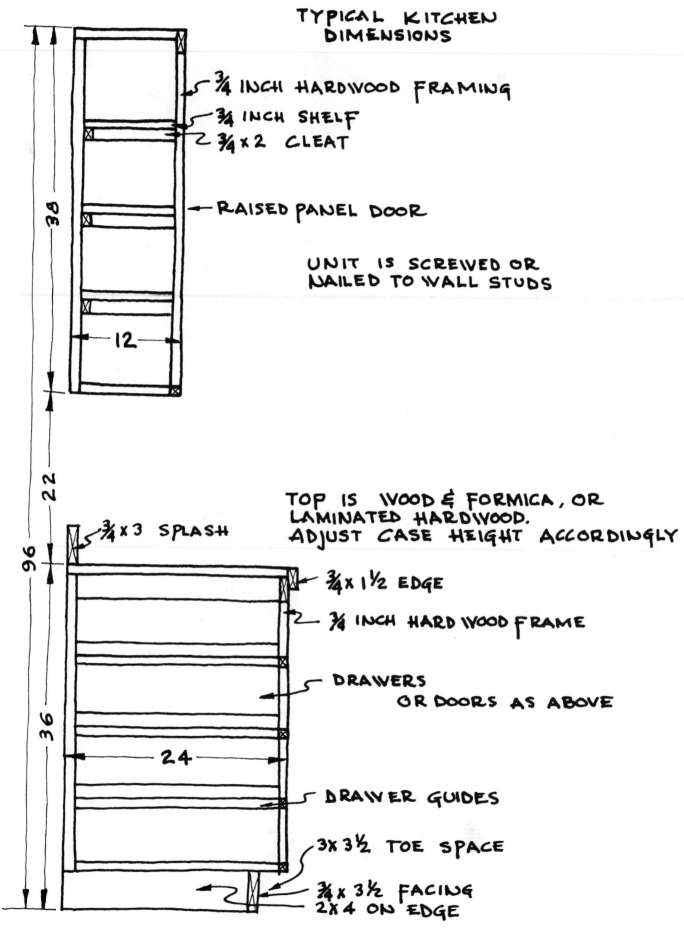

TYPICAL KITCHEN
DIMENSIONS

¾ INCH HARDWOOD FRAMING

¾ INCH SHELF

¾ X 2 CLEAT

RAISED PANEL DOOR

UNIT IS SCREWED OR
NAILED TO WALL STUDS

38

12

22

96

¾ X 3 SPLASH

TOP IS WOOD & FORMICA, OR
LAMINATED HARDWOOD.
ADJUST CASE HEIGHT ACCORDINGLY

¾ X 1½ EDGE

¾ INCH HARDWOOD FRAME

DRAWERS
OR DOORS AS ABOVE

36

24

DRAWER GUIDES

3 X 3½ TOE SPACE

¾ X 3½ FACING
2 X 4 ON EDGE

Kitchen Cupboard Adaptation

This efficiency kitchen is built in red oak, with an off-white plastic counter-top, and the interior is painted a gray-blue. Doors and drawers are built according to the patterns set forth in Chapter 4. Using this method, kitchens can be designed to fit any space and be of any size without resorting to plywood or particle board. Here one is limited only by his imagination.

Shaker Pegboard

In new construction, if real plaster is used, pegboards can be mounted directly on the rock lathe and be recessed as pictured in drawings 1 and 2. This method corresponds to the way horizontal pegboards and chair rails were installed years ago. If drywall construction is used, or if the board is to be applied to an existing wall, then the simplest method is surface mounting (3). It is best to paint or finish the boards before they are installed. Nails or screws should be filled and painted over. When possible, run the board completely around the room even if portions will never be used. This gives the boards an architectural quality and brings together doors, windows, and other openings. We usually mount the pegs before installing, and often the board has been painted. The pegs are treated in linseed oil only. Ordinarily, in a room having an eight-foot ceiling, the board should be mounted at about 78 inches from the floor. Remember to place pegs where clocks, mirrors, and pictures are to be hung.

WALL PEG BOARDS

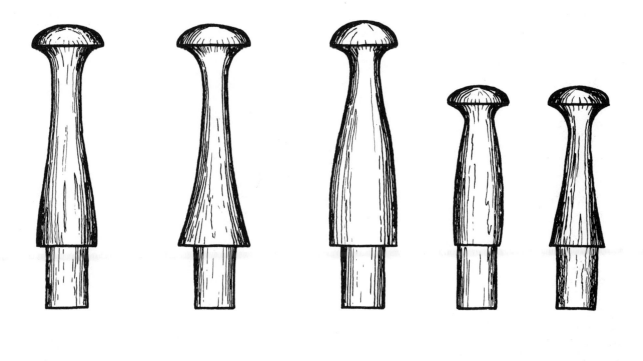

PEGS CAN BE SPACED 8 INCHES TO 2 FEET APART,
DEPENDING ON INTENDED USE

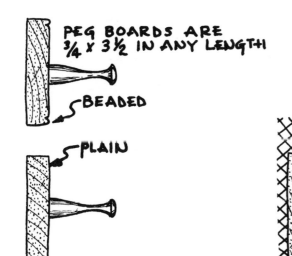

PEG BOARDS ARE
3/4 x 3 1/2 IN ANY LENGTH

BEADED

PLAIN

PEG BOARDS CAN BE MOUNTED
FLUSH WITH PLASTER (1) PROTRUDING
1/4 INCH (2) OR DIRECTLY ON
EXISTING WALL (3)

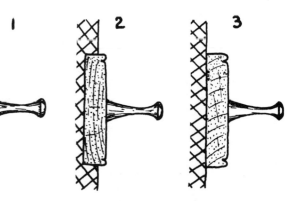

1   2   3

BIBLIOGRAPHY

Andrews, Edward Denning, and Andrews, Faith, *Religion in Wood*, Indiana University Press, Bloomington, Indiana, 1969.

_____, *Shaker Furniture: The Craftsmanship of an American Communal Sect*, Dover Publications, Inc., New York, 1937.

Bealer, Alex W., *Old Ways of Working Wood*, Barre Publishers, Barre, Massachusetts, 1972.

Blackburn, Abraham, *Illustrated Encyclopedia of Handtools, Instruction and Devices*, Simon and Schuster, New York, 1974.

Campbell, Robert, and Mager, N.H., *How to Work with Tools and Wood*, Pocket Books, New York, 1971.

Cescinsky, Herbert, *The Gentle Art of Faking Furniture*, Dover Publications, Inc., New York, 1967.

Constantine, Albert, *Know Your Wood*, Charles Scribner's Sons, New York, 1975.

Daniels, George, *How to Use Hand and Power Tools*, David McKay Co., New York, 1966.

Edlin, Herbert L., *What Wood Is That*, Viking Press, New York, 1969.

Fales, Dean A., *American Painted Furniture, 1660-1880*, E.P. Dutton and Co., Inc., New York, 1972.

Feirer, John L., *Cabinetmaking and Millwork*, Charles Scribner's Sons, New York, 1973.

Forbs, Reginald, et al., *Forestry Handbook*, Ronald Press Co., New York, 1955.

Gamon, Albert T., *Pennsylvania Country Antiques*, Prentice-Hall, Inc., Englewood Cliffs, New Jersey, 1968.

Gibbs, James W., and Meader, Robert W., *Shaker Clock Makers*, National Association of Watch and Clock Collectors, Inc., Columbia, Pennsylvania.

Greenlaw, Barry A., *New England Furniture at Williamsburg*, University Press of Virginia, Charlottesville, Virginia, 1974.

Gustanson, Ragner, and Olson, Ollie, *Creating in Wood with the Lathe*, Van Nostrand Reinhold, New York, 1967.

Hand, Jackson, *How to Do Your Own Wood Finishing*, Harper and Row, New York, 1968.

Handberg, Ejner, *Shop Drawings of Shaker Furniture and Woodenware*, The Berkshire Traveller Press, Stockbridge, Massachusetts, 1973.

Hayward, Charles H., *Cabinetmaking for Beginners*, Drake Publishers, Inc., New York, 1971.

_____, *Woodwork Joints*, Drake Publishers, Inc., New York, 1970.

Johnson, Theodore E., and McKee, John, *Hands to Work and Hearts to God: The Shaker Tradition in Maine*, Bowdoin College Museum of Art, Brunswick, Maine, 1969.

Joyce, Ernest, *The Encyclopedia of Furniture Making*, Drake Publishers, Inc., New York, 1973.

Kettell, Russell H., *The Pine Furniture of New England*, Dover Publications, Inc., New York, 1956.

Kirk, John T., *Early American Furniture*, Alfred A. Knopf, New York, 1970.

Klamkin, Marian, *Hands to Work: Shaker Folk Art and Industries,* Dodd, Mead and Co., New York, 1972.

Kovel, Ralph, and Kovel, Terry, *American Country Furniture*, Crown Publishers, New York, 1965.

McIlhenny, Henry P., and Madeira, Louis C., Eds., *The Philadelphia Museum Bulletin: The Shakers: Their Arts and Crafts*, Volume LVII, Number 273, Philadelphia, Pennsylvania, 1962.

Margon, Lester, *Construction of American Furniture Treasures*, Dover Publications, Inc., New York, 1975.

Meader, Robert F., *Illustrated Guide to Shaker Furniture*, Dover Publications Inc., New York, 1972.

Mercer, Henry C., *Ancient Carpenters' Tools*, Bucks County Historical Society, Pennsylvania, 1975.

Nutting, Wallace, *Furniture of the Pilgrim Century*, Old America Co., Framingham, Massachusetts, 1924.

_____, *Furniture Treasury,* The Macmillan Co., New York, 1962.

Ormsbee, Thomas H., *Early American Furniture Makers*, Thomas Y. Crowell Co., New York, 1930.

_____, *The Story of American Furniture,* Pyramid Books, New York, 1962.

Pain, F., *The Practical Woodturner*, Drake Publishers, Inc., New York, 1974.

Panshin, Alexis J., et al., *Textbook of Wood Technology*, McGraw, Hill, New York, 1970.

Salomonsky, Verna C., *Masterpieces of Furniture*, Dover Publications, Inc., New York, 1953.

The Shaker Quarterly, United Society, Sabbathday Lake, Poland Spring, Maine.

Shea, John G., *The American Shakers and Their Furniture*, Van Nostrand Reinhold Co., New York, 1971.

_____ , *Colonial Furniture Making for Everybody*, Van Nostrand Reinhold Co., New York, 1964.

Sloan, Eric A., *A Museum of Early American Tools*, Ballantine, New York, 1973.

_____ , *A Reverence for Wood*, Ballantine, New York, 1973.

Walton, Harry, *Home and Workshop Guide to Sharpening*, Harper and Row, New York, 1967.

Watson, Aldren A., *Country Furniture*, T.Y. Crowell, New York, 1974.

TOOL SUPPLIERS

Woodcraft Supply Corp.
313 Montvale Ave.
Woburn, MA 01801

Silvo Hardware
107-109 Walnut St.
Philadelphia, PA 19106

Woodcarvers Supply Co.
3112 W. 28th St.
Minneapolis, MINN 55416

U.S. General Supply Corp.
100 General Pl.
Jericho, NY 11753

Brookstone Co.
16 Brookstone Bldg.
Peterborough, NH 03458

Garrett Wade Co., Inc.
302 Fifth Ave.
New York, NY 10001

Frank Mittermier, Inc.
3577 E. Tremont Ave.
Bronx, NY 10465

Minn. Woodworker Supply Co.
Rogers, MINN 55374

Hiram Smith Whetstone Co.
721 Hobson Ave.
Hot Springs, ARK 71901